# THE BROKEN SCAPEGOAT

## From Trauma to Triumph

### Dee Dee Moreland

DH Book Consulting & Publishing
McDonough, Georgia

For information about special discounts available for bulk purchases, sales promotions, fund-raising, and educational needs, contact DH Book Consulting & Publishing at info@dhbooksandpublishing.com or www.deemoreland.com.

Published by DH Book Consulting & Publishing
100 Postmaster Drive #3235
McDonough, GA 30253
www.dhbooksandpublishing.com

Cover Design by Shan Mark
Photography by Destiny Moreland

Printed in the United States of America

First Printing: 2020

ISB: 978-1-7334436-4-7

# DEDICATION

With deep gratitude I dedicate this book to my Lord and Savior Jesus Christ, who breathed life into my lifeless soul and spirit and commanded it to live again!

To my husband Lamar, two sons, only daughter and grandson, who are the reasons behind my why!

# Acknowledgments

This book was literally birthed from the womb of trauma. However, God ordained it to be the perfect backdrop to bring massive healing to my broken soul with an intentional plan to use it to set others free.

I express my sincere gratitude to my husband, Lamar Moreland who held it down at home, encouraged me when I wanted to quit and coached me back to focus. Every time!

To my only daughter Destiny, and two sons Draveon and Dralon, you're one of the reasons why I'm still here to tell my story. I never thought I was good enough to be a mom, then you arrived. I've never been the same.

To my mom, thank you for allowing God to use you as a vehicle to get me here. Dad, thank you so much for planting the seeds of entrepreneurship in me.

To Lewis and J.D. Richards, my first big brother and sister in the Lord, thank you for accepting me as your "Lil Sis" when I was a mess!

Karmen Moon thank you so much for being one of my greatest supporters and assisting me during one of the toughest seasons of my life!

To Carolyn Brown, my sent Naomi, thank you for filling me with Godly wisdom and teaching me as my spiritual mom. You will never be forgotten!

To Kisha Sims, thank you for showing me what godly reconciliation looks like and all the laughter we could handle. Love you to life!

To Herman and Val Driskell, thank you for welcoming me into your life, home, and place of business. I'm so grateful for you for being my safe place so many times!

Renee Kendall thank you for introducing me to your crazy cousin, my husband. Thank you too for sharing your father who prophesied our marriage, hope we've made you proud in heaven, Leroy Kendall.

To Pastor Collette Gunby, thank you for teaching me foundational truths of God's word, accepting my husband, and keeping us accountable. I love you!

Last but not least, to my Apostles LaBryant and Phineka Friend, thank you for giving me language to find my identity, destiny, and call. I'm truly honored to serve under your leadership!

# Foreword

Our childhood is the first episode in a series of events that shape our mindsets and framed our lives. *The Broken Scapegoat* is an open invitation into the life of our leading lady, Dee Dee Moreland, as she discovers that her past subpar existence was a direct result of her parents' deeply rooted pain.

If you have ever questioned if you are good enough or smart enough, follow Dee Dee into the pages of this riveting saga, so that her life experiences can encourage you through Jesus Christ, to turn your trauma into triumph.

-J.D. Richards
Minister, Sister-Friend
Founder, ExpozurDreams

# Table of Contents

Introduction ..................................................................................... 1

Chapter 1 ........................................................................................ 3

In the Beginning...it Was Good ........................................................ 3

Chapter 2 ...................................................................................... 11

Something is Just Not Right! ........................................................ 11

Chapter 3 ...................................................................................... 17

The Struggle is Real .................................................................... 17

Chapter 4 ...................................................................................... 25

Not Seen nor Heard; Unprotected! .............................................. 25

Chapter 5 ...................................................................................... 29

Life Altered Forever .................................................................... 29

Chapter **6** ................................................................. 33

My Hero: Dad .............................................................. 33

Chapter **7** ................................................................. 37

Pleasing Mom: Impossible! ..................................... 37

Chapter **8** ................................................................. 43

I'm Not What I've Done! ........................................... 43

Chapter **9** ................................................................. 49

Another Major Blow ................................................. 49

Chapter **10** ............................................................... 53

The Great Escape ...................................................... 53

Chapter **11** ............................................................... 57

A Little Beacon of Light ........................................... 57

Chapter **12** ........................................................ 69

*Traps* ....................................................................69

Chapter **13** ......................................................... 97

*The Plot Thickens* ...............................................97

Chapter **14** ......................................................... 101

*A Divine Setup* ...................................................101

Chapter **15** ......................................................... 109

*My Naomi Gave Me Life* ....................................109

Chapter **16** ......................................................... 121

*The Reality of My Brokenness* ............................121

Chapter **17** ......................................................... 129

*Unmasking the Real Me* ......................................129

**Chapter 18**............................................................................ 143

*The Purpose of it All* ...................................................... 143

**Prophetic Poem**.......................................................... 151

# Introduction

I had no idea that something was after me from the time I was in the womb until my preteen years. I knew something was wrong, but I had no clue what that something was. For years I longed to make my mother proud, to be celebrated for my achievements and supported in my disappointments and loved unconditionally.

There seemed to be no rationale or resolution to this complex phenomenon, called parental narcissism. From a child's perspective the nurturing connection from a mother to a child is automatically expected. This is assumed even if the child isn't completely aware that it is necessary for their life development.

Emotional abandonment, detachment, rejection, disconnection, and word curses, to name a few, was the perfect breeding ground for emotional abuse. I spent years trying to gain the approval of my mom. I spent decades wondering why I was never good enough for her, trying to fix, adjust and even change out of desperation for her acceptance. But nothing worked.

After the profound revelation from the Holy Spirit, I realized it was not me but a deep dark bloodline toxicity that no one can see with the naked eye. Narcissistic abuse is hard, but parental narcissism has its own distinct hardship.

This book is intended to open the eyes of many who are unaware of narcissistic abuse running rampant in family bloodlines. I also aim to bring attention to the victims of this abuse to making them aware that abuse is not okay — no matter who it comes from.

This book is not written to dishonor, but to bring deliberate attention to this invisible wound. The identity of many in the family tree are being annihilated before they even become aware of their God given destiny as a result of this wound.

So, join me as we journey through the pages of my life and witness how this subtle, manipulative spirit manifested and the damage it does. Let me show you how you can overcome it and live a life of wholeness.

# Chapter 1

# In the Beginning...it Was Good

Born in the sixties and an only child, as a grade schoolgirl (as it was called back then), I can vividly recall having both my parents in the home and seemingly happy. My parents were raised in the deep southern parts of Georgia, but once they both finished high school, they moved to Atlanta for better opportunities.

My father entered trucking school and started his own trucking business. My mother was hired as one of the night-time telephone operators at one of the major telephone companies at the time. My parent's fresh careers provided well for the family. I have memories of going to church dressed from head to toe in ruffled dresses and socks with matching purse and gloves. I can remember holidays being a grand spread of food, gifts and toys for me and other family members. I attended a prestigious private school most of my early school years and participated in ballet along with other activities. I had the best clothes. We had numerous cars — from Cutlasses to Cadillacs to motorcycles to antique vehicles in our driveway. I can remember the day we moved into a house with a lot of land that included a variety of fruit trees —apple, pecan, muscadine and pear trees — and as they produced in their season I would eat from each one of them. I never got hungry while playing outside because I had much fruit and nuts to fill me up along with water from the hose streaming with fresh cold water. You may remember those days.

During those times, in my young mind, I had nothing to fear or fret about. My parents did very well as a young couple, in their early twenties, coming from the country to the big city. Back then, as an African American family in the '60's and '70's, my parents owned much, which was unheard of during that time. So, the picture of life for me at that time was normal and, in my mind, that was how all people lived.

Business was doing so well with my father's trucking business. With my mom working as well, we were able to afford relocating to an even larger suburban neighborhood where the homes were spacious, and even larger lands. The houses, in my mind, looked like huge castles. My dad was able to purchase his own Mack truck by then, and it had a bed in it which was my favorite spot in the truck. He cut out the middleman and used his own truck to obtain big contracts hauling from one client to another. We were blessed beyond measure and things seemed great!

As we quote quite often, "A picture can speak a thousand words." so as one would picture this story in their minds, you would automatically assume this is a life many unfortunate children and families would love to have; a life filled with joy and security. How many know that pictures (outward appearances) can seem one way and really be another or can start out one way and become another? As I grew older, around eight or nine — the age where you're really trying to find yourself what you like and don't like, discovering new ways to wear your hair, looking for the tangible hugs, kisses, affirmations, talks, acceptance, etc. from your mom — I slowly started to realize that there was something really dark hidden behind the walls of what I thought was a good and safe family life.

I began to desire a deeper bond with my mother. But instead of our bond growing deeper, I started to receive unloving outbursts of yelling, distance, and angry tones from her for no apparent reason. Over time my sunny life began to grow dim and gloomy with less hope for an answer as to why was this happening and why she was treating me so distantly. As a child you're depending on your maternal influence — your mom — to help you navigate through the phases of life and encourage you to be who God created you to be. Your mother should be one to somehow show you a picture of what life looks like for a female child. You automatically expect tenderness and great support; even if it was demonstrated by a hug or laying in her chest for comfort but that was not the case at all.

My picture of this great and protective mom was rapidly diminishing day by day.

My dad was my hero, and of course I was a daddy's girl. However, he had no idea of the new reality I was living in while he was out on the road making a living; or at least I thought he did not. Each day became filled with the immense harshness, commands, and slave-like orders from mom; so confusing and demeaning until I began asking myself, as an eight or nine-year-old kid, "What did I do to deserve this?" "Why is this happening?" "Why doesn't she love me anymore? I wanted to change in any way I could just to have her acceptance. I began to internalize and tried to rationalize what was happening. I thought that if I just won her approval and do something great or clean up to her satisfaction, that would make her happy and things would be alright.

After being in the new home a while I would wake up and lie down thinking, "What is going to be the challenge and "put down" today?" I used to think that if I just crept quietly, I could stay out her way. But I was totally unsuccessful. Mind you my mom never used profanity at all, but the tone and disconnect I felt through how and what she said, began to scream disapproval and rejection to me.

As time progressed, I felt more and more confused. I would wake up and hit the floor running with intensity just to make sure I spent time with my dad every morning before school. I stuck to him like glue. He was my safe haven and I was his little shadow he called "little stanker". I didn't know what it meant or where it came from and didn't care; that nickname made me smile. He would say it as he picked me up and swung me around in a circle until I was almost too dizzy to stand up. I would laugh until I could hardly catch my breath. My mom would be in the kitchen smiling while my dad was still present which gave me the impression things were okay and she must be fine. Once my dad left, and it was just us, the atmosphere of the room would become stiff and cold. I would be so afraid and confused, unsure of her mood. In one moment, I thought things were good. In the next I had no clue why or how I was the target for her frustration. In my little mind I would say, "Just do exactly as she says and there will be no problem." Or I would say to myself, "I'm going to give my mom a hug, maybe she's having a bad day." Sometimes I decided to just stay in my room to myself. None of these seemed to work.

Whenever she called my name, the fussy scream would be filled with sounds of dissatisfaction, anger and "you're in trouble for something" type of tone. I would hurry to put my uniform on, get my lunch box and hurry to the car so I could escape to school— the place where I found refuge during the daytime. On the way to school there would not be much two-way conversation or none at all. If she said anything it would mostly be about not getting my clothes dirty, sit at the front of the class because that's where the smart people sit, don't lose your sweater; don't, don't and don't.

When I arrived at school, she would breakout with such a grand smile and pleasant voice to all who she would engage. This confused me even more. But, being the child that I was, I brushed it off and proceeded to embrace laughing, talking and learning with my friends while at the same time having a deep sense of all kinds of "whys" in my head about my mom's back and forth behavior toward me and how different it was when conversing with others.

At the end of my school day, I would always start feeling antsy and not know why; but I did recognize that the tightness and fearful feeling escalated then. As soon as the car drove up, I would be so excited to tell my mom about my day and what I did, but instead I would hear negative toned questions like, "What do you have for homework? What kind of grades did you get? As soon as you get home get your bath, do your homework and get ready for bed!" Whenever I did show her some of my work, she would say a quick, "That's good." or "You could've done it like this or that." So, I wasn't really sure whether it was a compliment or a disappointment, or both. Nevertheless, I did what was commanded every day before my dad arrived.

My mom held a tight and strict ship when it came to household chores. They had to be done to her standards, which seemed impossible most times. But I would get them done, nevertheless. Whenever I would hear my dad's truck driving up the driveway, I would feel a sense of instant relief. He would be so exhausted some days until he could barely make it to the back door. I would stand at the back-garage door waiting impatiently for him to turn the key and open the door. No matter how tired my dad was he always took a little time to give me his full attention; he would embrace me with the biggest hug and kiss. I would help him bring his things in and follow him like his little shadow. My dad would then speak to my mom. She would respond, but it seemed to become more and more distant and dry as time progressed. I'm not sure why that was but I knew it started to be the same way as she responded to me almost every day. I could tell that my dad started noticing that something wasn't quite right, but he never said anything about it in my presence. Something dark was brewing silently as time progressed.

As I was turning ten, emotional ups and downs had become commonplace between my mom and me. On my tenth birthday I was shocked to find out that I was going to have a baby brother. I was going to experience what life would be like having a sibling. My parents were overjoyed, and I would have someone to play with. Being an only child for ten years can cause you to become settled with being alone and entertaining yourself. I was great at it but unlike some who grew up as an only child, I wasn't selfish. My mom always drilled the attribute of sharing in me and she did not have it any other way!

As the time drew near for my brother to arrive on the scene, I remember being excited to see what a baby looked like— not realizing I was once an infant too (laugh out loud). What should I expect? How do I help as a big sister? All this uncertainty and excitement was running through my little mind.

I can't remember too many things that happened during my brother's infancy and toddler stage, but I do recall taking pictures; with he and my parents, and him being such a plump and juicy baby with a grand smile.

Fast forward to where my brother was old enough to run up and down the hallway of the house making crazy sounds — as brothers do — and me yelling at him to be quiet. Of course, he didn't listen. He sometimes annoyed the heck out of me by coming in and out of my run attempting to tear the heads off my dolls and you know I had a real problem with that. I was a very neat person, and everything had its place. I'm not sure if that was part of who I was, or because of my mom's dissatisfaction with things being out of order; either way it became a part of me. Of course, this type of behavior between siblings is quite the norm and we would have quite a few of these spats back and forth. There were days we got along well and then there were days I wanted to just lock him outside and pretend I didn't know he was out there. Whenever we would have these disagreements it would usually be because of him coming into my room and taking stuff and my mom would intervene. Of course, it would almost always be my fault and I would be punished for it.

At first, I thought it was normal, but it began to intensify. I wasn't sure why, but I knew the harsh difference my mom would make between my brother and I wasn't right or fair. Even though I loved my brother to the moon and back, I started noticing how my mom handled me in comparison to my brother; she was indifferent to me. This just added to my confusion.

# Chapter 2

## Something is Just Not Right!

My family believed in celebrating the holidays and special days; birthday celebrations, and summer vacations. We would take road trips to my maternal grandparents. I loved that trip. It was a four-hour trip and we would stop at corner stores and pick up snacks. We made this trip many summers and I looked forward to seeing all my cousins— my mom's sister's children — as well as some of my dad's family; they were from the same area in South Georgia. We would all arrive the same day or sometimes a day before or after each other. I don't know about anyone else in the pack, but the highlight of those yearly trips for me was talking and listening to my granddad's stories of how he grew up.

There's one particular trip I will never forget, I'm not sure what year, but we were on the way to my grandparents, maybe an hour prior to arrival. I can't remember why my dad was driving another car, a Cutlass in particular, but as we followed behind I remember seeing my mom looking down for a second to insert an eight track tape (some of us remember that era) and the car suddenly swerved off the road. She jerked the car back to get back in her lane, but it hydroplaned into the air, flipped about six times, and landed in a church yard upside down while the wheels were still spinning. We had just stopped at the gas station to fuel up and get snacks. When we landed, I vividly remember my honey bun still in my hand while I was strapped in my seat belt. I was calm and smiling and engaged in eating my honeybun (when I tell you that honeybun was good to my soul), as my dad rushed to the doors of the car. However, the doors were jammed so he proceeded to kick the back window out to pull me out first. I could hear my mom screaming profusely as dad tried to release her from the car, but I think the fire department had to cut her out. We had a few scratches but no serious injuries. I overheard my dad telling emergency personnel that he looked into his rear mirror and the car was floating in midair, hit the ground and flipped. I can tell he was upset but relieved that we were okay. From that day forward my mom never drove on expressways even though the accident hadn't occurred on the expressway; it was an old two-lane country road. I guess that it affected her psychologically, I'm not sure. I learned later that was a miracle from God that we were still alive! As I recall, we were treated at the hospital and released to continue the trip to my grandparents.

My grandparents, Jo, and Pat occupied this small quaint home, it was a simple brick home with mint green trimming around it at the time, one little window air conditioning unit in the living room. The house had three small bedrooms and one bath— yes one bath and we all had to make it work. Each year as we arrived, my granddad Jo would be waiting for us on the porch or walking around the front yard until we drove up and scattered out of the car like insects; especially when my cousins arrived the same day.

My mom had a large family; there were ten sisters and brothers but the oldest died before I was born; so, you can imagine how many children there were which made it even more fun. As we came in, Grandma Pat would have fresh baked cakes and pies waiting for us; if you know genuine country folk, there was always a meal cooked and ready to serve to whoever would drop by... That's just how that southern hospitality was expressed.

After greeting everyone and bringing in all our bags I ran out the door with speed right into the arms of my granddad. I guess he reminded me of how my dad interacted with me. We always stayed at least a week and I recall playing hide and seek, hula hoop, kickball, jack stones (the authentic ones), softball and anything else we could think of in the scorching heat.

Each morning I would hear granddad Jo rise early while everyone else was asleep. He would put on his overalls and whistle or sing under his breath while he walked down the hallway toward the kitchen. He brewed coffee, ate breakfast, and prepared to get on his tractor to drive into town. But he would stay all day until almost night. I would think many times as the evening approached how in the world grandad can see how to farm anything in the dark. But I quickly figured out that granddad Jo was staying away hoping grandma would be asleep by the time he got back home so he wouldn't have to endure the high pitch screeching sound that came from her. In the midst of him preparing to leave in the mornings, I would hear my grandma yelling, and I'm sure others heard her as well. The tone would be ear piercing but familiar. Hearing this, I tried to sort out in my mind what in the world could she be yelling and fussing about so early in the morning. I thought maybe he had done something awful, but it seemed to just be the normal way she addressed him.  It was like he was immune to it. I remember her saying:

"Jo, where are you going this early?"

"You know these children are here!"

"What's wrong with you?"

"You ain't going in my car, drive the tractor!"

I wondered about that for a long time; was she angry with him? Did she not love him or just didn't like him? It was confusing but familiar —when he left, she began singing wonderful hymns, smiling, and proceeded to cook breakfast for all of us like nothing ever happened.

It reminded me of the pattern my mom and I had. That that was scary to me, but I would find a way to quickly switch my attention to something else.  I didn't know what to do with those negative thoughts and feelings that were constantly festering in my mind, so I chose to focus on having fun.

During our stay, one of my uncles had a convertible and he would take all of us, his nieces, and nephews, to Ms. Cross's corner store to buy us all bags of goodies. Most times my mom would be the only parent to say I couldn't go. My uncle in turn would ask her why; she could never give a sensible answer. My grandma and aunts would all ask why. Again, she could never give a reason. I would be so disappointed and embarrassed. My excitement would dwindle to an instant inner sadness and borderline anger. My uncle would still snatch me up and put me in the car with the rest of my cousins and drive away. My emotions were all over the place trying not to allow it to affect me, but it did.

This would happen many times during our stays and someone in the family would periodically come to my defense without knowing the depth of how broken our relationship was. My dad would witness this all the time and would turn a deaf ear to it; rarely coming to my rescue.

As the sunset painted the evening sky, I found myself every evening sitting near the front door anticipating granddad Jo's arrival on the tractor. Some days he would come before we retired for the evening and some days he wouldn't arrive until way after. The nights he arrived before we retired for the night, he would entertain us by playing his harmonica or watching WWW (Worldwide Wrestling). "Wrestler #1", "Tony Atlas", "Andre the Giant" and "Thunderbolt Patterson" were his favorites. They owned a small black and white television in the family room and grandad Jo would be yelling and beating the floor, jumping up and down cheering for his favorite wrestler to conquer his opponent. You could never, ever tell granddad that wrestling wasn't real; that that would be an all-night debate, so we just let him live in his world. After listening to several songs on the harmonica, watching, seemingly twenty wrestling matches, we ate dinner and crashed for the night.

I would see my mom embrace my cousins — conversing with them about school and telling them how smart they were — and I would try to follow suit expecting the same embrace, but I received the exact opposite response from her; no conversation and no warm embrace. My mother treating me this way was becoming more and more a problem for me. Why was this happening to me? I felt a little relief when my other uncles witnessed the way she treated me differently, but no one really addressed the issue head on. It was just observed and brushed off like it had never happened. I knew for sure there was something definitely dark and wrong. I still tried to think positively because it was always drilled into me, by my parents, to honor your mother and father or your life would be cut short. I absolutely hated this scripture because it was used as a manipulative tactic to control me with guilt, fear, and condemnation. Every time I heard them use it, it always left me feeling like I was in an emotional prison trapped between honoring my parents and the feeling of a young orphan girl who was full of life and personality linked with a deep longing for the approval and validation from her mom and now her dad. I lived in the snare of feeling like I had to do everything just as they said, or God would-n't be pleased with me; I lived in constant, inner anxiety.

As our vacation week with the family would come to an end, it was time to face the reality of going back home knowing what I had to experience almost every day with my mom. As my dad loaded our bags into the truck, I cried. I didn't want to leave. I was surrounded by family, but my greatest sadness was leaving my granddad Jo. I loved him so much and, in my heart, I desperately wanted to stay with him for the rest of my life. I knew that wasn't going to happen though. I dreaded to go back to the norm.

# Chapter 3

## The Struggle is Real

Around age thirteen, I was trying to understand this adolescent stage of life; my body seemed to be going haywire. I had many questions swimming around in my head that I desperately wanted to ask my mom but was afraid to. During this time, my father was ordained from a deacon to an associate minister, in a small little country church in which we attended every Sunday like clockwork; whether you wanted to or not you were going.

My mom dressed well, sang in the choir and was the treasurer, but she ruled with an iron fist when it came to image and how we looked outwardly. Everything had to be coordinated — from the top of our heads to the soles of our feet. I remember when I was way younger, she would dress me in ruffled dresses for church with most of them having a small bell sown into the dress at the bottom; every time I moved it rang. My mom would go to the West End Mall to shop for me every year for Resurrection Sunday. I had matching ruffled socks, purse, shoes, gloves & handkerchief. I also, remember my brother being dressed in a blue sailor jumpsuit one year, with a matching hat with a red bow tie. That should give you a clear picture of how serious she was about her dressing ministry.

And don't let it be a piano recital or a recitation! She took it went to a whole other level!

As a teen my interests started changing. I started wanting to experience different looks with my hair, desired to visit with friends my age, and go to the school games, etc. Well the real struggle began: the struggle between learning my identity versus my mom desiring to live vicariously through me; the struggle of trying to find out who I really was as a developing young lady seemed unreachable; and the struggle of trying to bloom the right way verses fighting to get out of the emotional and psychological prison I was in.

Standing outside one day, bored out of my mind, I noticed that our neighbor had a niece, about my age, move in with her. I was ecstatic just to see someone my age! I ran into the house to ask my mom if I could go and meet her. The first thing out of her mouth as usual was "No!" I asked her why? I told her that I didn't have to go *in* the neighbor's house I just wanted to kind of hangout, talk, and get to know her while standing in the driveway. Her reply was still "No and because I said so!" I stomped outside, filled with anger and frustration. This was the main reason why I loved school; it was a way of escape for me. I loved my mom and was desperate for some physical show of affection and understanding from her. This desire started diminishing day by day.

I had many friends in school and was a straight A and B student. My friends would talk their plans for the weekends and would invite me to all kinds of events, but I could never go. Why? Because my mom wouldn't allow it. Anger, and now resentment, began to inwardly intensify. It happened so often that my friends just stop asking me. I became that friend whose mom was like Pharaoh. My school days would be filled with laughter, fun and clowning around in between classes but once I got off that bus, my emotions would shift like gears on a truck.

A close friend who lived on the opposite end of our street invited me to her home one day. My mom had met her parents during a school function, so I took a chance and asked could I ride my bike to my friend's house for a while (it was still okay back then to ride your bike somewhere without being too concerned about being snatched). She said yes, but to my surprise, she was only allowing me to go for only forty-five minutes to an hour. In my mind I was like, "Forty-five minutes?" It would take me fifteen minutes to ride to her house and I had to be back in the house within that time frame? It was unfair, controlling, and didn't make any sense to me.

When my dad came home that day, I told him what happened, not for him to take sides, but to bring fairness to this struggling relationship. He did attempt to inquire about it, but she couldn't give a legitimate answer; just went on ranting to avoid dealing with the issue at hand, so nothing was really resolved. My grades were great, the dishes had been washed, my bedroom cleaned, the bathroom straightened, so what possible reason did she have for never wanting me to connect with others and just be a happy young lady? Her rules felt like I was always in a strait jacket — strict and non-negotiable. It felt like she got pure pleasure in rejecting me because she knew she could control me; she was the parent and I was the child.

She was suspicious and tight about everything. As long I wasn't engaging with others she was satisfied and disregarded the fact that I had become the prisoner in this scenario. This became a hidden, vicious, and volcano-type cycle waiting to erupt. When it came to others, especially children, she was like night and day. She would embrace them and speak in such a pleasant tone until I was totally convinced that either I was crazy, or she was. This struggle was truly real and full of uncertainty.

There were days she came home from work and there would be one dish in the sink — all hell would break loose! There would be yelling, nagging, and fussing that seemed never-ending.

I would stay in my room preparing for the next day, trying to drown her out and she would come in my space and say things like:

"Are you wearing that?"

"That is not what you are supposed to wear."

"I know I taught you how to dress."

Or another one was, "My co-worker's daughters dresses like… why don't you wear what they wear?"

The subliminal message I heard loud and clear was that I was never good enough and can't make some decisions on my own. As a teenager I was no longer interested in dressing like a little girl but now wanted to wear age-appropriate attire. Fashions changed and I wanted to wear jeans and a t-shirt, not blouses and dressy pants, to school. We would have miniature battles often because she was bent on forcing me to adopt an image that she had for me. We never had an encouraging conversation about what I wanted to wear or how I liked to style my hair and we figure it out together.

I finally realized I wasn't going to be understood so I succumbed to changing my clothes, many times, after she left to go to work and changed them back before I returned home. I was a very jovial person, but I was also shy, so I never desired to have all my "goods" hanging out. Some days I was successful at changing clothes, and some days I got caught.

Whenever that happened my mom couldn't wait to tell my dad; however, she would often blow things all out of proportion. Of course, I would be punished, and she would sit on the sofa with a half-smile on her face. My heart would be crushed because my dad, my protector, whipped me for sneaking, but he never really asked me about the reasoning behind my actions or had a real discussion about it. Punishing without any real conversation behind it is abuse period! It is like backing a cat into a corner and it begins to swell and hiss. This kind of parenting often opens the door to unintentional rebellion.

In order to participate in some of the activities at school I joined as many extracurricular activities as I could, such as the marching band and the drill team with the hope of not only being able to participate, but I made sure I join the ones where attendance was part of my grade. That way she wouldn't reject my joining. I noticed she didn't seem to put up too much of a fuss about that and I didn't figure out why until later. My mom was addicted to image. How others viewed her was extremely important; so, whenever I performed it was about how good she looked as a mom and not necessarily because she supported her daughter.

I overheard her several times on the phone telling others how great I was and bragging about the awards I had received, but I hardly ever heard it from her directly. Now this only added to my confusion. At first, overhearing those comments about me coming from her was an encouragement and made me think that maybe I was gaining her approval. I felt that I would finally have an open door to talk to her about girly stuff: how to deal with that time of the month, what age could I date, how do I respond to boys, etc.... maybe it was a breakthrough. Unfortunately, I finally realized though that my accomplishments were really more about her and her image, and not me. It was a disappointing blow and complete let down as a young girl who was longing for the authentic attention of her mom.

My hope of ever bonding with my mom was very bleak. The emotional struggles between us grew stronger and more distant every day; it bled into the whole family structure. My dad would come home almost daily to a yelling match between the two of us. My brother would be stuck in the middle not knowing what to do. You could sometimes hear us from the beginning of the driveway up to the back door. My dad knew deep down that the relationship between his wife and daughter was in deep trouble. I think he just didn't know what to do. So, he avoided it altogether.

My mom started lashing out at him and treating him in the same manner as she did me. She became nagging and unpleasant to be around; she would speak to him in a such a demeaning tone and there was never a way to satisfy her. Most times she would have a frown on her face which displayed dissatisfaction; never seeing it from someone else's view had become her coping mechanism. I wracked my brain trying to figure why I was so problematic to her.

I was always vacillating back and forth, desperate for answers no one could give me. What I did know, was that I was the blame for everything, and it was no longer alright with me.

Mind you, the outside world of family and friends had no clue that there was a major emotional cancer growing in our family. We had the facade of being the perfect family which only made me angrier and flustered because I knew the truth; we needed help and neither of them were willing to admit it. They did whatever to protect the false image of it all. The struggle was definitely real; if you can imagine fighting something you know is present, dark, and powerful, but you have no idea how or what to do about it. This is a perfect picture of fighting aimlessly at something you know is trying to kill you!

# Chapter 4

## Not Seen nor Heard; Unprotected!

Having parents who grew up in the south and who firmly believed a child should be "seen and not heard", "don't speak unless spoken to", "you're a child you don't have an opinion or a personal thought about nothing", shaped my mindset of being a slave. Subconsciously, it taught me that I shouldn't be "seen nor heard" nor that it mattered. It taught me that my voice didn't exist and that my perspective wasn't important. Unfortunately, it also taught me to seek attention and help elsewhere.

By the end of my ninth grade my family was trapped in our own personal prison of image, pride, and denial. My grades began to drop which brought on more stress as I became even more withdrawn and isolated at home. My mom had attended college for about two years and was unable to finish because she got pregnant with me. She had been extremely studious in school so in turn ruled with an iron fist when it came to her children earning straight A's and B's. Her approach was very intimidating and harsh when it came to helping me with homework, so I no longer looked forward to doing it. Doing it had become drudgery and no longer fun to learn. She made me feel slow, dumb, and stupid because of her hoovering over me yelling "How can you not know that?" or "We just went over that!"

She probably meant well, but that did not help me understand why she kept dishing out high doses of disapproval toward me. Many parents who parent in this manner, well intentioned or not, have no idea why they cannot connect with their children; even when they become adults. This type of emotional trauma does not disappear just because your children are now adults. Healthy discipline is one thing but toxic discipline breeds abuse, distrust, and isolation.

At this point my dad's reputation as a minister was on the line so he drifted into protecting it more than me, his "little shadow". This was the straw that broke the camel's back for me.

Being drawn into the pressures and reality of a "PK" (preacher's kid) on top of the strong narcissistic nature of my mom, my emotional state of mind was now locked in survival mode. Survival mode can work for you, or against you, and is often a dangerous state of mind because desperation creeps in on your decision making, your emotional state and your actions. Living in this state many times leaves you in even worse situations because there's no healthy rationality. "Just do my time until my release date and then my life will have meaning." is the mentality that now lives in the life of a child who have, or is living, under narcissistic parenting.

Mental depression started pursuing a relationship with me; life became numb. I knew little about myself and was totally green when it came to guys, dating, or what I should be looking out for in this world. The closest thing I heard about guys from my parents was "Keep your pants up, and your dress down!" I had no clue what that meant. Boys had begun to show interest in me, and I had no idea what not to do or what to do. Still the attention I had started receiving felt somewhat nice. I would hear all sorts of things in the girl's bathroom about what to do and not to with boys; some of it was interesting and some it was downright nasty to me. I would get teased often because I was still a virgin. I was about ninety pounds "soaking wet", skinny-as-a-stick and had a head full of thick long hair and big boobs. Ugh! I was considered by most of my guy friends as a little sister; they called me "short stack", or "little shorty" or "meat, meat" short for my first name. Even though school life gave me a sense of relief temporarily, I had given up hope on ever being understood by my parents — especially my mom. I thought I still had my dad's support but that even started fading away with him trying to keep what he thought was peace with my mom. I eventually totally disappeared into the background of his life.

Mom's disposition had grown saltier as the months went by. The bickering between she and my father or the verbal spats she started with me had become a way of life. It was just a huge pile of hidden mess.

Whenever we had company over, the atmosphere was almost hilarious. You would've thought they were the best Christian couple there was on this side of glory. Don't get me wrong, they were great providers as I stated before, and they loved doing for others, but the relational connection within the home was almost nonexistent. My dad would tell some of the funniest stories of how he grew up and would have everybody cracking up. My mom would burst into laughter as well and I'm looking at them like, "Who are you people? Really? Am I hearing and seeing things? I must be in the wrong household." After company would depart or before they would arrive, it was like being in a funeral home.

# Chapter 5

## Life Altered Forever

I can't quite remember what season it was, but an older relative, named Ray, came to visit with us from out of town on a short trip. I wasn't ever clear why he came, but nevertheless he was there. I remember him arriving and don't remember much after that. That night he stayed at our house changed the course of my life forever. We all had dinner, talked a bit and my mom showed him the room where he would be sleeping during his stay — which was the far bedroom, my baby brother's room, down the long hall toward the front of the house. My room was midway in the hall and my parents' room was the first large bedroom entering the hall. My dad always secured the house before he retired for the evening and that was the last thing, I remembered hearing before I fell off to sleep.

I'm sure it was late in the night when I felt something touch my legs. I thought I was dreaming but as I continued to feel the touch, my covers were pulled back at the same time while I was being gently shaken awake. I was half asleep and half-awake, and attempting to open my eyes when I heard a quiet whisper saying, "Come with me." while shushing me to stay quiet. I recall wearing a long pink-and-white-printed gown on with flowers and ruffles on the edges. It was dark as I was drawn away from my bed, pulled to the back bedroom, and laid on the floor. That's when I realized it was my relative, Ray. In my young mind, I was still trying to figure out what he wanted. He began to fondle me as he pulled my underwear down. I felt what he was doing but I wasn't sure what he was doing or why; it felt strange and creepy. It felt like a slow-motion film or an out-of-body experience. I finally came fully awake and began to push him away, but he was too strong. I was never taught what molestation or incest was, so I didn't recognize either. I remembered my dad telling me not to sit on a man's lap, but I was never told what that meant. As he became persistent and continued trying to force himself on me, the light came on. It was my mom. Back in those days parents checked the house during the night. However, I was usually unaware because I was always asleep by then. She saw him on top of me, caught him right before he totally violated me, and yelled for my dad. I was shaking like a leaf and felt paralyzed. I can't even remember whether he said anything or not. I was numb for what seemed like hours. I felt traumatized. I thought my mom was calling my dad to help me, and for her to give me some clarity as to what was happening or call the police or something.

Instead, I got the shock of my life; the ultimate let down a young girl (child) could ever hear from her parents! My parents started shouting at me, asking me with anger, and in a shocked tone:

"What did you think you were doing?"

"You're so fast and grown!"

"Why did you do this?"

I was in total shock! I was the victim! I was their daughter who had been violated! They never bothered to ask me what happened or how I was feeling. I don't remember them asking him anything. If they did, I just don't recall. There was no comfort, protection, or nothing of the sort. I couldn't believe my ears. I frantically tried to tell them what had happened — that he had come into my room, but I couldn't get a word in over them shouting at me.

That was the night I was forced to keep my mouth shut and never tell anyone. I was bullied into silence. It was expressed in a threatening way which magnified even more fear, trauma and confusion and sent a clear message to me saying, "If I can't depend on my own parents to defend me, who can I trust?" I ran to my room for refuge and cried the rest of the night.

The following day nothing was said about it and he was gone. Just like that. It left my emotions swimming in a lake of guilt without a lifejacket. The confusion that calibrated my mental state was unbearable. Their dejection left me questioning myself to the point of no return. No counseling. No discussion. No closure. Just forced to conceal a terrible and dark family secret.

My view of my parents changed forever after that incident. Any little expectation I had left, withdrew from my hope bank, and left my emotional and psychological account in the negative from that day forth. I remember so clearly the message playing in my head, repeatedly, "You don't matter, and your voice don't matter." That was the day I no longer felt "seen nor heard". My inner girl faded away into darkness and transformed into "THE BROKEN SCAPEGOAT".

# Chapter 6

## My Hero: Dad

The next day I woke up like a zombie; pressing to put one foot in front of the other. I can't remember if it was a school day or not, but I knew another layer of my reality had been revealed. I was faced with the reality of how, I could no longer hope for any emotional protection from my mom. But the kick in the gut was I could no longer expect it from my hero, my protector, my all in all — my dad. It was such a shock to me how he believed what my mother said over what he saw. It was if we never had a bond; like I was a stranger who violated his home. What was even more frightening to me was I now had NO protection or a place of refuge. It was gone!

The male, my father, and the male, my relative both crushed the little hope I had left to dust. My spirit no longer had a pulse, I was still fun-loving on the outside but there was an empty darkness on the inside. I felt the ultimate emotional and now physical betrayal and abandonment. I felt more devastated from my dad's failure to come to my rescue than I did from the heinous act itself. I felt exposed, dirty, ashamed, and guilty as if it were something, I had done to bring this on myself.

My mind became flooded with escapism and seeking places of relief, emotionally, anyway I can get it. I was confused as to why. Why did he allow this to happen? Where was he when I needed him? Why didn't he show up for me? He was there when it happened. I thought he loved me. Why did he always take my mom's side? What about me? All of this continuously raced through my head. So, I pressed my wrecked emotions deep within me and wore the shame and guilt as a garment.

The idol of image (that's when how it looks is way more important than how it feels and how it is), had consumed both. From that day forward the reality of their strong dysfunctional and narcissistic close-knit bond that nobody could penetrate, opened my eyes wide. My brother was the only one that seemed kind of normal and that's because he was young and had no idea what was going on. This was a good thing, I guess.

I finally realized who really ran the show at home; my mom. I just didn't realize how toxic it was until I saw him crumble under her will and joined forces with her when I was violated. I had no idea at the time what this kind of dysfunction was, but I knew it was wrong and unfair treatment. My dad was a decent hard-working man who found himself caught in a web of an extremely controlling wife he loved but who emasculated him. He found her difficult to live with, and so the best way he could try to keep peace in the marriage was to play the role of "go along to get along". That grew into a whole different branch of coping mechanism; enabling. Mom was the boss and he accepted it by withdrawing and avoiding the big elephant in the family. His little girl, his only girl, his "little shadow" no longer was his priority; pleasing mom at all cost was the main vein that fed his insufficiency to step into his authority as the head of the home.

As time passed, I witnessed repeatedly, that his needs were not a priority and he accepted my mom's behavior no matter how it infected us or the atmosphere of the home. He did all this just to keep her pleased and so he didn't have to hear the constant bickering, even though it was a temporary fix. My mom seemed to be on a mission to sabotage the father-daughter relationship. We would be playing a game together or watching our favorite TV show and she would often bring a negative vibe in the room by sitting with a displeased look on her face or demanding that I go do some chore that wasn't up to her standards; right in the middle of our interaction.

My parents had an unspoken and silent agreement between the two of them that was like a reinforced steel wall. It gave off an obvious vibe that you were not welcomed in their inside world, especially daughters of narcissistic (over-controlling) mothers. I was her daughter by blood only, but in reality, I was her competition. But I had no idea why.

Daughters who are parented under the dictatorship of a narcissistic mother, is always viewed as a threat; the daughter reminds her of herself. A daughter should never have to compete with her mother for a spot in the family; its eccentric and toxic. It became a tug of war to gain any attention from my dad. She would never verbalize it, but her actions were clear to him as well as to me, who was running the ship.

My emotion was a revolving door. Some days I would try to come to my dad's rescue because I felt so sorry for him as she would talk to him like he was her child. There were times I was embarrassed for him and other times I was so full of hurt, pain and agony as to why he allowed her to reign and control not only him, but me as well. I was so conflicted because he always told me the man is the head of the household. However, that is not what I experienced. The mixed messages were so confusing and unclear. From day to day you never knew what would take place which clearly showed the emotional health of our family was on life support.

Again, the only thing I was scolded and beat over the head with was "Honor your mother and father; that's what the Bible says!" I heard that scripture so much, that the older I got the more I hated it with a passion. I know that doesn't sound spiritual to you religious buffs, but it was the truth; it made me angry every time I heard it. Whenever mom would be on my back about every little thing, dad would demand me to just, "Do as you are told! You're so disobedient and rebellious!" That was far from the truth at the time. I guess he was trying to get brownie points with her by rejecting me and never giving me the opportunity to share my side of any issue. I really loved my dad but as the "broken scapegoat", the reason why everything was wrong in the family — anger, resentment, and distrust — festered and eventually overtook the precious and fun-loving bond we had together.

# Chapter 7

# Pleasing Mom: Impossible!

M om, was publicly viewed as a kind, giving and helpful person, and she really was! She was not only an excellent baker but a great cook. She baked for people at church, for the sick, for times of bereavement, on her job, for birthdays and holidays. She really had a niche for making simple and great tasting homemade cakes and other deserts. As I stated before, she kept an immaculate conservative home as well as living up to her image of a well-dressed preacher's wife. She worked her way up from a telephone operator to an engineering drafting clerk at the phone company she retired from. She conversed with her siblings almost on a weekly, if not daily, basis. She was a caring woman who would comfort the weak, make constant phone calls to the sick if she wasn't able to visit them, mailed birthday cards and performed an array of other benevolent acts of kindness. So, you see, outwardly she was a highly respected and sweet church-going woman who loved God and loved people.

On the other hand, the private life of mom, the side of her no one — and I mean no one — knew about, except the ones who lived under the same roof was the complete opposite. Mom had a sometimes bitter, unpleasant disposition almost daily. The atmosphere of the home was like walking on a tightrope praying not to fall because if you did the consequences would be fatal. When she would call my name, it would strike through me like a clash of lightening, the sound always sounded like she was displeased and angry with me. It was high pitched, similar to Loretta Divine's voice in the movie "Kingdom Come" *laugh out loud*. I was in constant mental agony, straining my brain trying to figure out why was she so angry all the time. What she considered instructions, were really dictations and orders. Her words toward me truly felt like orders from a warden; harsh and stern. But the most confusing thing was when people would visit or the phone would ring in the middle of one of her rants, she would answer it with such a meek, kind, and proper voice. I never knew which side of her would come out; none of us in the house.

I often felt like I was the reason why my mom hadn't finished college because she was pregnant with me. I felt like she wanted to make me pay for it for the rest of my life. I held that weighty guilt for eternity, seemingly. She tried to mold me into the shape of her dreams and aspirations and lived inevitably through me. When I took the route of entrepreneurship it made her even angrier with me.

Entrepreneurship ran heavily on my father's side of the family, so it was no surprise that a desire to become a master cosmetologist was my goal in life. I was absolutely fascinated with cosmetology because it allowed me to express all the creativity that was bottled in me. Becoming a cosmetologist also meant that I would have an opportunity to make great money, meet many different people and do something to unlock me from the emotional prison I was in.

But, not surprisingly, my mom was not trying to hear anything about my goal of becoming a hairdresser. In fact, she told me one day that I could never make money in it, that I was going to college and that was final. I made several attempts to explain to mom that I had no desire to attend college so please don't waste her money sending me. I didn't do well in those type of environments. I was barely making it out of high school at that point. What did she do? She enrolled me anyway.

It was the most miserable experience of my life. I attended for about two quarters and I couldn't do it any longer. I decided to leave and pursue what I wanted for the first time in my life. This caused huge arguments and barriers when it should have been a time of support and joy about where I wanted to go in life.

The latter part of my junior year in high school, I bloomed out of that skinny little girl into a fully shaped young lady. I remember how frantic I was about everything that came with it. I tried talking to my mom about it, but that was a nightmare. I definitely couldn't go to my dad with it, he wouldn't know what to tell me, so I was left to find out on my own. On my own, I picked up advice — good and bad — from overhearing conversations from girls in the bathroom and some from my friends. I didn't have a secure and confident self-image at all, even though the fellas would give me compliments. I didn't have a clue how to act or receive them so I would just say thank you, nervously.

My newly developed body drew attention to me from the boys that I wasn't ready for. In a way I liked the attention but, in another sense, it made me uncomfortable because some teased me about my breast. That totally freaked me out. So, to soothe my anxiety of being teased and feeling violated, I became known for wearing jackets all day until I returned home. Some guys were pleasant and easy going and some were just jerks.

Prom time was approaching, and I was asked to the junior prom. I was kind of excited that someone wanted to take me to the prom but fearful at the same time because I knew asking my mom about participating in something of that magnitude, especially with a boy, would be like climbing Mount Everest with shorts on; an impossible journey with a tragic end. I told him honestly, "You might want to ask someone else because my mom is very strict, and I don't want to ruin your prom on the account of me and these crazy rules." He persisted and I got up the nerve to ask, fearing rejection the whole time. Once I asked, of course there were a million and one "ifs", "ands", "maybes", "I don't know yet", "ask your father", etc. Some questions I expected; my reason why I gave her all the details beforehand.

Later, other guys asked me out too and I tried to do the right thing and asked them to come meet my parents. But it was always something wrong with everybody, so I just stopped asking. It was about a week or two before the prom and she still hadn't given me an answer. It was like waiting for a parole release; at this point I was like, "Can I go or not?" It made me angry because I needed to tell my potential date in time just in case, he needed to take someone else and so I wouldn't be embarrassed about it. It was like mom's controlling spirit would take joy in making me sweat and wait until the last hour. To my surprise, she allowed me to go.

I wanted to go but was hesitant because I never got to enjoy events and outings out with my girlfriends; my early curfew times and rules had me watching the clock constantly. For Prom, I got my first feathered haircut and she bought me a beautiful dress. I had a great prom evening. Some of my friends were so surprised to see me there because they knew how my mom was. These were the same friends who invited me to places, but I was never allowed to go.

At prom I overheard other couples planning to go to after parties and hotels to hook up and drink. I had already told myself if my date suggested going to a hotel with him, he would have hell to pay. That was the furthest thing from my mind because of what had happened to me in my past. But I didn't have to worry about that; he was a perfect gentleman the whole night. It felt great escaping to a different atmosphere with people my age and having fun.

As my curfew drew near, I started getting anxious. I was so worried about getting home on time, he had to console me and reassure that he would get me back. I literally began to sweat and have heart flutters. We arrived about ten minutes after curfew. He walked me to the door, kissed me on the cheek and waited until my mom opened the door. She spoke to him in such a pleasant and thankful tone. But as soon as he drove off, she slammed the door and started yelling like Sergeant Carter on Gomer Pile. I said, "What is the problem. I came back only a few minutes after curfew. "What is the big deal? Traffic held us up a little." She acted as if I had stayed out for five days. My dad tried to intervene, but he couldn't get a word in and eventually faded into the background as usual. The whole night was ruined for me.

I made a promise to myself that when I graduated, I was out. I was going to leave home for good — never to return. If I had to sleep under a bridge at least I wouldn't be treated like a criminal.

## Signs of a Narcissistic Mother

Over time, I realized that I was dealing with a narcissistic mother. This mother is controlling, lacks empathy, lacks maternal nurturing, treats you as a project, is totally self-centered (unable to see things from another point of view), allergic to correction and/or judging or examining themselves but are prone to judging in others what they refuse to see in themselves. She's always right and everyone else is wrong, highly defensive, super secretive, worships image, is addicted to being right, threatens to withdraw — sometimes with unspoken words, very hard to please, knows no boundaries, a skillful manipulator, deflects (never takes responsibility for their actions) and is over indulging in her adult children's life.

## Effects on the Daughter/Child

As a result, this type pf relationship has an adverse effect on the child's psychological and emotional well-being. Just as I was, this child is usually starving for approval, seeking to be nurtured, never feeling good enough, always confused, and indecisive. This child is manipulated constantly and made to feel that her needs are never important while being constantly rejected. She is always seeking approval and validation from her mother, but in turn she is left feeling guilty and ashamed. Criticism seems never-ending. As a result of the mother's jealousy and always competing with her daughter, that daughter becomes an extreme people pleaser.

# Chapter 8

## I'm Not What I've Done!

O ver time, the temptation of escaping became extremely intense. I began to rebel and the craving for love and attention woke up in me like never before. It was like something came over me. I never desired to disobey my parents, but I felt pushed into a corner and I was fed up. I needed to feel loved, supported and cared for emotionally. I didn't quite know what that looked like or felt like, but I was willing to try something other than what I had experienced all my life. In the past I brushed off guys because I was afraid and uncertain about what they would do to me. I was controlled by fear, abandonment, heart wounds, anxiety, worry and now lust. This type of thinking and desire opened a wide door for me to enter and explore a territory I knew little to nothing about. I became promiscuous. My purest hope and surety were to have someone who would love and accept me, but in return I received great disappointment and more emotional and psychological abuse. My thought pattern was, if I give boys what they want, then I would receive the same in return. I quickly found out how that was a lie from hell wrapped in deception.

During the last two years of high school, I had multiple sexual encounters. I found myself trying to heal an open wound I'd had since childhood and one that had gotten worse, after I was sexually violated and blamed for the act. As a result, I gained a reputation of being loose and free. By that time, I didn't know how to stop it. I felt it was too late. There was such a yearning in my wounded soul.

I began to sneak boys in the house while my parents weren't home. I would stay after school for activities but would find myself elsewhere, with the wrong guy doing the wrong thing. My grades had taken a plunge from A's and B's to D's and F's and even zeros. My demeanor and attitude changed. I became rebellious against her prison-like parenting and began to verbally challenge (not disrespect but defend myself) my mom in order to get her off my back. I was trapped in what seemed like an emotional abyss; on one hand I developed suppressed anger and on the other hand I was afraid to speak up for myself due to being controlled by that one scripture, "Honor your mother and father! Honor your mother and father!" I absolutely had no problem honoring them but, in my head, I would ask God, "Is there anything in the Bible to protect and direct parents from damaging their children? Are we supposed to just become the slaves and doormats of our parents until we are grown?"

I genuinely wanted to please my parents and God, but the message was delivered and embedded with such an intimidating, fearful delivery. This caused me to view God as this big, bold voice waiting to send me to hell if I didn't do everything my parents told me. The question I had was, "How do you honor dysfunction and abuse?" Is that what God required from children and never addressed the parents about anything? This thought pattern toward God became the lens in which I viewed and approached God; through fear, punishment and being hard to please!

The funny thing about that is whenever I spoke the truth about how phony the family was, and that the facade they put on was a joke, it would infuriate them both. They didn't want the secrets of the house to leak out to family or friends; even though these were the same parents who taught "the truth will set you free".

I, being labeled as the *scapegoat*, learned to just wear the label of being everybody's excuse for why things are wrong in the family. Because I was living it, I walked out the definition of a scapegoat. Scapegoats (black sheep, misfits, outcasts) are the ones who ask the uncomfortable questions that nobody wants to answer. They are the ones who want to know the "whys" of a situation: Why am I your excuse for your wrong choices? Why don't you want to talk about the real truth? The scapegoat becomes a threat, in their eyes; a threat of exposing what happened was terrifying for them.

It was never my intent to get revenge; all I wanted was a mentally, emotionally, and spiritually healthy family. I just couldn't grasp why that was so hard for them. Normally, when people, especially children, experience emotional, physical, or psychological trauma it causes them to withdraw, rebel or both. It is the equivalent of being trapped between facing the consequences of exposing the secret(s) and carrying the heavy guilt of being the reason for breaking up the family. They learn to medicate the wounds of their souls in many ways in order to cope with life. Often, it can be extremely destructive and imprisoning.

Something had turned on in me that I couldn't explain nor control. I found myself experiencing bouts of depression and not feeling valued. The more I sought love, the more I found myself drowning in the depth of lust. Validation and the longing for acceptance and love became my addiction but I wasn't even aware it was happening. My addiction had sub counterparts: over-pleasing people, feeling needed, perfectionism, anxiety, suicidal thoughts, never feeling good enough, insecurity and feeling devalued. I developed a "taking what I can get" mentality.

This kind of mindset will project behavior that you assume is your true identity. It's a deceptive lie from Satan and when you come into the knowledge of the truth of who God says you are, then revelation begins to teach you "I'm not what I did". Oh, I admit I've done many shady and shameful things, but when I began to learn that God never views us in the now but always speaks to us from our future, it was freeing. He sees us from his image not our own. Outward appearances can be so very deceptive and would cause one to quickly judge someone while they are in the pit of life. I've been guilty of this in the past myself due to my PK, religious upbringing, and narcissistic nurturing. But God has delivered me from a somewhat condemning view of others. When the light of the truth of God is shone on your mess, there's absolutely no room to judge others. Even as believers we erect a judgmental mindset by thinking now that we aren't engaged in our prior lifestyles or if it wasn't your particular struggle, then you demonize what you don't understand or have an answer for. Where they are today in their process is not an indication for where and what the future holds for them.

By my senior year of high school, I'm ashamed to say, I was executing a plan to leave home just to have a chance for some peace of mind. I never desired to live a wild lifestyle and I didn't for the most part, but my grades declined so much that I didn't know whether I would graduate or not. My mom wasn't having that, so she navigated me through the process. She didn't want to be shamed, which is the only time she showed up for me when it had something to do with making her shine and not out of real concern.

# Chapter 9

## Another Major Blow

Shortly after my senior year my paternal granddad came to visit. He was such a kind, orderly, sporty dressed and poised man. I didn't know him well because he lived in another state, so I didn't get to see him much. His second wife's side of the family lived in Georgia and had moved not too far from where we lived.

During one of several visits and fellowships, I met a nephew on his wife's side of the family who was around my age. He subtly pursued me, letting me know that he wanted to get to know me. Well, his family did not seem to mind that much. As time progressed, we began to see each other often. I can't remember if he came for the summer or he had moved with his Georgia family temporarily, but somehow that longing for love and attention drew me closer to him and his attraction drew him closer to me.

Eventually we secretly started having sex. His family nor mine had any idea.

As time passed, I began to feel sick and I had no cycle. I was pregnant! I was terrified. I didn't know what to do. I didn't even know who I was, so the thought of raising a baby was scary. Scariest for me though, was having to tell my parents. Oh my God!

His family was upset but was willing to talk and work it out. I desired the same even though I didn't know "much about nothing". Well when it came time to tell my folks, the crap hit the fan! As expected, they were upset, screamed, yelled, blamed me, but for just one moment I had hoped maybe they would embrace my baby. I hoped that after they calmed down, they would be open to talk about it, maybe console me, even if it was only because I was carrying their grandchild.

Turns out they knocked me down with another major blow to my already broken and hijacked emotions. They weren't willing to talk about it at all. They never asked what I felt about it, what options we could use, what the pros and cons were, nothing but angrily shouting "We don't want it and it's not coming here!" Those words resonated in my soul for years. I had a hard time shaking those words out of my spirit.

A few days after the big blow up, silence, avoidance and alienation became my parents' coping mechanisms. I would hear my mom whispering on the phone, so I would stay to myself in my room terrified, wandering where my life would go from there. Thoughts of suicide began to crowd my mind. I wanted to just kill myself so that the mental torment will be all over.

That same week, my mom told me to get dressed and that I was going out with her friend so she can take me somewhere. I thought it was so strange to send me with her friend and she not go, what was up with that? Well, that somewhere, to my surprise, was an abortion center.

I heard of the word, but I had no idea what it was or what people did in those places. That should tell you how naive I was. I don't remember having much conversation from my mother's friend, but I vividly remember being ushered in this cold-feeling facility, much like a small hospital. I remember looking back at my mom's friend waiting for some type of explanation as to why I was here and why my mother didn't come.

It finally registered what was about to take place when I was again ushered into another room, given some brochures on abortions, and instructed to undress and told that a doctor will be with me in a few. If I could have jumped out a window I would have, but there were none. At this point I was crying profusely, feeling violated all over again with no choice in the matter.

Afterward, I never wanted to speak to my mom again. I wondered if my dad knew about this. If so, why did he allow her to do this to me? It didn't dawn on me until after my emotions calmed that he must have known something because I never gave birth to their grandchild. I had all kind of questions in my head about the guy's family. Did they have a say in all this? How did he feel about it? Did my parents even tell them about what they decided to do? All I remember is never seeing him or his family ever again. It was like they never existed. It was another blunt blow to my identity; another dark chapter in my life that left me emotionally scared, laying lifeless in a pool of my own blood.

From that day on, life for me was like the walking dead; you know you're breathing but you feel no life, no vibrancy. This is no way to live and something had to shift.

# Chapter 10

## The Great Escape

I finally graduated, barely, and I found myself facing the reality of leaving the only comfort I knew, and that was being with my friends and interacting with my teachers who loved me and embraced me with intentional encouragement. I was extremely saddened to see us all depart into our different pathways of life. During graduation I bawled my eyes out, and even though my parents and some family were there, they had no idea what the depths of my tears spoke.

A few months passed, and my mom's anger and displeasing attitude toward me magnified and I couldn't take it anymore. It was time to go! Prepared or not, I couldn't live under the pressure of our dysfunctional facade any longer. My dad wanted me to just adapt to her the way he did, but I couldn't do it. I talked to him again and again about what I had to go through when he was out working. It was her word over mine every time, so I never mentioned it again. Months passed and home life was pretty much the same old routine. I thought if I could just survive until an open door came for me to pursue my dreams of being an entrepreneur and support myself at the same time, I would be well on my way to learning how to navigate in the world on my own.

My mom had a beautiful soprano voice and sang in the choir for years with the same church friends since I was a young child. Among the several friends she had, there was one friend in particular whose son was getting married, and mom was ecstatic. My mom would visit her and vice versa. I knew her son because we both grew up in the same church and he was a little older than I. During one of the visits to their home I met the son's fiancé', Sandra, and we seemed to hit it off almost immediately. We conversed about things pertaining to the wedding, the wedding date and how excited she was about everything. Sandra's persona was so inviting and full of wisdom. She later married and had a grand wedding. It was exciting to see it all unfold. They moved into their new home and began to settle in as newlyweds do.

I would often visit as we became more and more acquainted. Eventually a new bond formed, and we became close friends. She would share with me how close she and her siblings were growing up, being close and supporting of one another. She had a sister who lived out of state and a brother who was in the military.

One day, her mother-in-law came to visit while I was there. Somehow the subject came up of how I should be introduced to her daughter-in-law's brother. I didn't think much of it, but it was quite flattering. She began to bring out pictures of her family, including her brother Chris. Hearing the comments about each picture and their history was refreshing. But I could not delete the picture I saw of her brother out of my mind. He was so handsome!

A few months later, Sandra called me to tell me her brother was coming to visit from the military and invited me to come over to dinner so we could meet. Sandra's mother-in-law, to my surprise, asked my mom if I could come over to visit while Chris was there.

I was utterly shocked. He came, we were introduced, and the rest was history.

We hit it off and began to write each other, became good friends and it grew into a great relationship. Whenever he came to town, he would take me out, but of course I had to struggle with my parents, mainly mom, about letting me go out. I was a few months shy of nineteen years old and she still fought to keep me confined to a little prison. I was so frustrated with her and upset every time he would come to town because she really never liked anyone who got close to me or looked like they would help me become a better me. Chris offered to come meet my parents as a respectful young man would do, but they were never interested. So, I stopped asking them.

Well this particular time, I told Sandra I couldn't take it anymore and she encouraged me that things will work out and if there's anything she could do to help let her know. Sandra was always a listening ear and I thanked God for her. She always looked at things from all perspectives. I called her one day and asked her if she would help me find a place to live. Unexpectedly, she offered her home to me and I melted into a bag of tears. I was overwhelmed with surprise. She and her husband agreed that it would be okay.

I never thought it would come to that, but I packed only the things I had purchased from working a small part time job, which consisted of my clothes and shoes and some other small items. I wrote a note to my parents the night before letting them know I was safe. I didn't tell them where. I did let them know that I never intended to hurt them, but I could no longer live a lie.

The next day, I was nervous, but I knew I had to face my fear of leaving if I was going to be an independent adult. I had never been given the chance to show my parents just how mature I was, naive in some areas, but mature in most. My mom was that mom who was always scared to live and scared to take a chance on something. Everything had to be planned, and if anything deviated off the plan she couldn't function. After being raised under this kind of anxiety and fear, it bled into my identity and I didn't even recognize it.

When my brother went off to school and our parents had left for work, I placed my things at the edge of the garage and waited for Sandra to pick me up. She arrived just as she said she would. We loaded up hastily. As we drove down the long driveway, in my heart I knew I would never come back to live under this emotional bondage again! It felt liked breaking out of prison and entering a life of open opportunities. I was so grateful to Sandra and her husband for giving me the one chance that I needed to jumpstart a life for myself.

I felt physical freedom, but emotionally I was still broken and bound. I needed a safe haven to just breath and focus on who I was and what I wanted out of life. It was the perfect divine place in that season of my life. I grieved in my heart while my unclear future beckoned for me to pursue it.

# Chapter 11

## A Little Beacon of Light

During the few years I lived with Sandra, I accomplished quite a bit. I worked fervently, continued dating Chris, and God blessed me beyond measure. I lived with her when she had two of her three babies, and it was a pleasure knowing I could do something to return the favor. We were no longer just friends. Our relationship had evolved into sisterhood. I admired her so much because she taught me the basics of life. I considered her my new extended family.

She later helped me to build my credit so that I could eventually purchase my first car in my name. She was a wiz with finances, thank God!

Chris and I dated for about four years. He was a great guy and we started considering engagement, but our relationship dissolved over something that was out of my control. I had given my life to God and my personal convictions began to affect the way I viewed life. I was a babe in Christ. I didn't have the courage to tell Chris, and it hurt him when I no longer desired to do some of the things our relationship was used to. I was truly devastated over the breakup, but I thank God for the experience; I learned much from it. Chris later married and is doing well.

Sandra's family and I remain friends even to this day; she has and will always have a special place in my heart.

The time came for me to move. The family outgrew their home, and it was time for them to purchase bigger living quarters. I totally understood. I was then faced with looking for a place of my own and pursuing a life in the cosmetology world. Working in the field of cosmetology opened many doors for me to meet some amazing people.

God opened the door for me to rent a one room efficiency and you would've thought I lived in a mansion. It was tiny, but it was my own space and I could afford it. I didn't care about not having furniture or a bed or nothing for that matter. All I found comfort in, at the time, was that I wasn't living on the streets and looked forward to a new norm.

During this journey I met another amazing person who took my life to a new level; Dea. I met Dea while she was training under one of the greatest hairdressers in our era. Jean Smith was amazing, and she ran a tight ship. She knew her craft and she didn't play. She was the first black woman to win a Rolls Royce in the New York hair competition. She sold her Rolls and opened a salon called the "Rolls Royce Experience". The salon was decked with peach, black and white decor with elegant class displayed throughout the salon. I recall seeing this lady at the Bronner Brothers hair show back in the eighties and nineties. I knew I had to work with her. She possessed something I needed and wanted. But little did I know, she was a tough cookie to work under. Many people couldn't work with her style of tough teaching which included yelling, cussing and some-times embarrassment. I came to her salon asking if she would allow me to apprentice under her even though I had my license.

After several rejections, Jean finally said yes, and that was the beginning of my friendship with Dea.

She was a little older than I, but as we worked together, our lives began to merge, and I knew she possessed a stance in life I desired. Her persona was always full of confidence. We spent quality time together during and after work. During many conversations I began to share a little about my life and how I knew there was something better for me once I left home. She would always encourage me, and she helped me to believe in myself. Dea encouraged me to try new things, telling me that would be the only way to grow and cultivate my life. Wisdom would exude from her and it would draw me to want to hear more and more.

As we trained at the salon together, we learned some powerful techniques; like how to give quality results to our clients and work with a speedy grace. Jean taught us time management in a salon environment, which was her pet peeve, and rolling and blow-drying techniques that were never taught in school. Her methods were totally unorthodox, and when she came to check on her clients, it had better be done the way she wanted it, or she would let you have it right in front of the client.

I was so determined to stick it out and was rewarded by being promoted to her personal assistant. She saw something in me that I hadn't seen in myself. She did not believe in taking all night to get clients in and out. She ran the salon in two shifts, morning, and early evening; the salon would close for two hours during lunch which gave everyone personal time to run errands or have a decent lunch. After lunch, the evening shift would begin, and we would be out of there no later than nine p.m. The books would be packed with appointments. Clients came from everywhere in the city.

After a few years, the time came when Dea relocated to another salon. I was saddened but happy for her.

In the meantime, Jean continued to stretch me beyond my own perspective. She came in one day and told me I was being entered into the student hair competition at the Bronner Brother Hair show. I looked at her and thought she had been drinking. I was in total shock because that was the furthest thing from my mind. "Hair competition?" I asked Jean, "What do you mean?" Ignoring me, she never replied to any of my questions. She gave me the list of requirements, which included a live model where I had to create a daytime and evening look from the same roller set. I was like, "Are you kidding me?" As she walked away, she told me to clear my schedule and that training would start within the next few days. I had no words. I was totally baffled. Bronner Brothers back then was one of the top black-owned beauty supply businesses in the southeast.

I went home in total fear mode, but a whisper came to me and said, "There is something she sees in you and you need to let her help you bring it out." So, I embraced it. I trained twice weekly for five weeks. The judges were tough, and everything had to be on point.

Competition day came and I landed second prize in the Bronner Brother Student Competition that year. I was elated and so was Jean. It wasn't often you saw the pleasant side of her, but her heart was in the right place and she loved what she did. After that milestone it wasn't long before I followed suit in Dea's footsteps. I thanked Jean for pouring her knowledge into me, but it was time for me to move on as well.

I asked Dea if there were any booths available at her new workplace. There was. I was given an opportunity to rent a booth right next to her. I couldn't explain it, but I was drawn to Dea's spirit. It was so fresh and uplifting.

The owners of the salon, Jay and Viv, were some of the sweetest people I have ever encountered. I've never seen a couple work together and vibe the way they did. It was really shocking to me because in my mind, I only knew one kind of marital function and that was dysfunction.

Starting out I had no clientele, but the place just felt right. I would watch my sister-friend, Dea, work and I would overhear her sharing the Gospel of Christ with her clients every time she got a chance. There would not be a day go by when I didn't hear her loving on, encouraging or sharing wisdom from the word of God. My intent was never to be nosey. I was more drawn to what she shared with them than I was with the client's issues.

After work one night we went to eat, and I couldn't wait to ask her what was it about her that made her so different? She began to share her testimony with me, and I was blown away. I was glued to her from that day forward. I wanted to hear more and more.

At that time, I was still living at the efficiency apartment. One day I came home from work and the owner wanted to talk to me privately. I thought I had done something wrong but somehow, he heard that I had no furniture, bed or much of anything for that matter. He told me they had a brand-new bed, and chair for me.

On the same day, I got a call from my sister, Sandra, who I used to live with, telling me she had a sofa, kitchen items and bathroom decor to give me. I was totally tripping out that someone would just give me all this stuff while this expecting nothing in return. I was in tears of joy. I was so overwhelmed with the unexpected kindness that my mind strained to comprehend it. Mentally, I felt like I didn't earn it and I didn't deserve it. They insisted and I accepted. My history molded my thinking into "no one gives you anything. You have to do it yourself".

I later found out the owners of the salon where I worked, Jay, and Viv, were believers too. The love and care of Christ reigned in that salon. They would invite me over for meals, talk about how Christ changed their lives and how it was their mission to do the same for others. They had parties and entertained at their home constantly; Jay was an amazing God gifted chef. They all became my extended family. Even though I still had deep emotional wounds, it was such a breath of fresh air to be a part of a circle of people who didn't condemn me but loved me through my process.

As our relationship grew, I somehow ended up moving in with Dea. She lived alone and had an extra room. I was so grateful. Her home atmosphere was extremely peaceful. I could tell the peace of God lived there even though I knew little about it. I knew in my heart God was real but the only view of Him that I had was going to church, having long — and I mean long — revivals, collecting money to buy the preacher a better car and don't ask any questions about anything. Don't question God was one of many things I heard over and over. That was a snapshot of what I knew about God. Jay, Viv and Dea worshiped at the same church so they invited me to visit and boy was that another new experience for me.

When I arrived at *The Place of Grace* one Sunday, I thought they were having a concert because everybody was friendly, and the room was filled with joy. The sermon hit home with me so hard, I could hardly keep it together. "I mean surely these people aren't this happy, good grief!" I thought. I said to myself, "I'll come back another time and maybe the people won't be like this. Maybe it was just a hit or miss thing." As I visited more and more, from the praise to the message, it was like the pastor, a lady, was talking directly to me. I wondered had anybody told her anything, but I knew in my heart that wasn't true. One day the message was so intense with the spirit of the Lord it was like He pulled me from my seat and floated me down to the altar. That day I gave my life to the Lord.

I was so tired of the mental torment in my soul, I just gave it all over to him. That was truly the beginning of my life being shifted in a whole new direction. I didn't recognize it when I left home that day, not sure of where my life would end up, that it was God guiding me and sending me to people who loved on me, gave to me, encouraged me, opened their doors to me and assured me that God is the answer to all things.

Giving my life to God changed my life entirely. God had a plan for me. The more I engaged in the word of God the more I grew as a babe in Christ. My clientele seemed to grow overnight. I learned foundational truths about tithing and the grace and glory of God. I was consistent in my walk for a year or so and had a great support system, but I couldn't understand why I still faced unforeseen challenges, disappointments, temptations, and real struggles during my journey.

My perspective when I came to the altar had been, I gave my life to Christ and now it will be perfect with no problems. I quickly found out differently.

Unaware of my bloodline demons, they began to rise up not long after I committed my life to Christ. It seemed like all of hell came against me, and a war between my flesh (my will) and God's will (the Spirit) grew so intensely that I didn't have enough Word in me to combat Satan's snares. There were still some folks in my life that I needed to remove myself from, but I didn't understand why it was so necessary. They were friends who were decent people and we had some great times together; however, they were into some things God didn't want me to partake in anymore and this was a hard task for me.

When I found people, who seemed to have accepted me, I loved hard, and so when God began to come after the ungodly relationships in my life it was difficult. My perspective on that was so warped. I knew that certain persons weren't a good fit for where I was going, but I was afraid of being alone, so I felt that some company was better than no company. What a deception! I would try to please both, and as I did that, there was a daily enticement for me to go back to my old lifestyle. Eventually it worked. I was slowly drawn away from Christ and found myself tangled up in bondage again. I began to club again and flirted around with many different ungodly relationships in a determined pursuit for love. My emotional trauma was still very much alive, and through the open door of disobedience, Satan took the opportunity to draw me into an unholy lifestyle magnified times seven; worse than it had ever been.

Temptation (enticed by the bait) breeds deception (the lie) then disobedience is (conceived through impatience) and now *bondage* (the baby *sin* is born) *warning:* (ignorant or not) leaving from the covering of your Heavenly Father with the intent to run your own life leaves you exposed in the enemy's territory and his playground is saturated with grenades of unwanted consequences! (James 1:14-15)

My relapse took me on a journey of four years of being entangled with wrong men who would drain my emotions even more, and they took advantage of my needy appetite. My emotional trauma bled into all areas of my life. My desperate need for acceptance and validation always put me in positions to be used and taken advantage of by men and female friends. My thought pattern was always not to treat someone like I was treated emotionally and even though that was a great attribute to have, when it's exposed to toxic people it will derail and delay your life every time. My life became this one big huge web that I had no idea how to get out of.

Imagine the traps set for animals, after the trap bounds its subject there is no way of escape; the more they struggle to get out in their own strength the more entangled they become. They're alive but wounded. Broken and traumatized inwardly. Bleeding internally hoping to be rescued.

Luke 11: 24-26 *When the unclean spirit comes out of a person, it roams through waterless places in search [of a place] of rest; and not finding any, it says, 'I will go back to my house (person) from which I came.' And when it comes, it finds the place swept and put in order. Then it goes and brings seven other spirits more evil than itself, and they go in [the person] and live there; and the last state of that person becomes worse than the first.*

During my backslidden state I still kept in touch with my big sister, Dea, and extended family from time to time. I still needed them in my life but was ashamed of what I had done. To my surprise, they never stop showing how much they loved me and more importantly, how God still loved me. I couldn't wrap that kind of love around my brain. I expected to be kicked to the curb and rejected because that was what I was used to, but it was totally the opposite. They would tell me the truth in love but without trying to strong arm me with scripture. They prayed that the truth of the word would peel the scales off my eyes and that I would be compelled to come back to Christ wholeheartedly.

During this time, doing my own thing, trying to please both worlds, God and man, I always felt the tug of God compelling me to come back to Him; heard it in many ways and many times. I was on an undecided emotional roller coaster. One minute I wanted to surrender and next minute my flesh would rise in combat erecting its own agenda. Every time I remotely came close to making that decision to go back to God, Satan would always present what I call an "attractive distraction" to keep me on a path of self-destruction and deception, whether it be a girlfriend wanting to go to party or meeting a new guy who seemed to be into me, or keeping me distant from the people who God put in my life to help mature me along this journey.

A journey consists of longevity, not instant gratification. On a journey you will encounter many delays, disappointments, fears, distractions, and especially deceptive traps. Traps are set to bind its prey no matter what kind it is. Depending on what a hunter is hunting for, traps vary in size, shape, and structures but they all have the same goal in mind and that is to capture its prey, kill it, destroy it, and consume it.

# THE BROKEN SCAPEGOAT

Let me share with you a few of the traps Satan had set for me on my journey to victory.

# Chapter 12

## Traps

### Trap One

I traveled down many twists and turns in my life, on my way to authentic freedom and made some really jacked up choices. I walked right into various traumatizing traps. One of them was when I met an older guy who flattered me. He was calm and collected. I was so young and relationally ill-equipped in some areas. He wasn't a party person and lived a quiet and laid-back kind of life. I can't even remember where I met him. All I know is I met him while a close girlfriend and I were out one night.

We dated exclusively. I thought I was in love. After a short time, and I mean short, I found myself pregnant by him. I told him, thinking he would be there for me. But when I told him the news he was out like a car coming through the drive-thru window; entered my life, slowed down just enough to get his appetite fulfilled, and then drove away and left me to pay for the tab. He returned no calls and seemed to have dropped off the face of the earth.

Now I was faced with the same fear and torment I went through when my parents made me abort my child. I was abandoned all over again. My girlfriend Sha was there for me as much as she could. I cried uncontrollably and didn't know what to do. Immediately, out of nowhere I heard a voice clearly speak to me saying "just get an abortion. It's a simple fix". It brought back some gruesome and scary memories. I fought this voice for about a week, but regrettably I succumbed to the temptation and had another abortion.

Afterward, I went into a deep depression filled with guilt, shame, regret, unworthiness, loneliness, and another layer rejection.

I had given up on life and just couldn't understand why God would put me here just to be rejected. For some reason, through all of this I never became angry at God. I just didn't feel like I had a purpose of being. Those who have dealt with bouts of depression on any level knows that it's a very isolated emotional prison. You can be in a crowd but alone. It's a crazy, deceptive reality. Thoughts of suicide chased me for days and as I searched for ways to commit suicide, a thought came across my mind to call my big sister Dea. I mustered up enough strength to call her. When she answered I burst into a frantic cry. I could hardly get my words out. She had no idea I was contemplating suicide, and to this day she doesn't know (she will when she reads this), but God gave her the words through prayer to speak life into my empty and bruised soul.

I was still weak, but I felt better. After I heard her voice, for some reason, my desire shifted to wanting to live and not die. The guilt of having two abortions plagued me like a demon in the night, but by the strength of God I gained the strength to carry on.

By this time, I had moved several times. I literally felt like a vagabond. I existed, but never felt like I belonged. Even though God always made a way for me to have a roof over my head I felt like I was never settled or accomplished in anything. I was just drifting through life carrying this invisible bag of uncertainty. I fought the dark demon of mental torment like no other. I had fixed in my mind that I was unforgivable, and God was too angry with me to ever use me in any capacity. I came into agreement, unknowingly, that I didn't matter, and the background is where I belonged.

**Trap Two**

Another time during my uncertain journey, I landed my very first apartment in my name, woot, woot!! Having a place to call my own was a feeling of great progress. It was a rather large one-bedroom apartment and I was so grateful. I could finally breathe a little and felt a sense of accomplishment.

I called my best friend Sha and told her the good news. Shortly, after settling in, Sha and I began to decorate my place as best as we could. I didn't have much furniture, but I didn't care. I was just grateful. I learned by trial and error how to cook good southern meals such as collards, homemade cornbread, meatloaf, etc. I learned to pay bills and handle my small budget. Believe me, it was a disaster the first few times, but as I practiced, I was able to get it down to a science.

When Sha and I would hang together, our chronic laughter would dominate any atmosphere. Laughter was part of our DNA. We were like two peas in a pod; usually when you saw one you would see the other. We had met years earlier while working at

71

Dunkin Donuts and attending a vocational school earning our certification to become a master cosmetologist. We both graduated but while I pursued it, Sha had decided it wasn't her cup of tea. She was a beautiful, tall, mocha-shaded young woman whose personality exuberated a sensitive love for children, but also contained a bulldog's strength when it came to defending someone she loves, as well as herself.

Sha was in a relationship with her boyfriend since high school. We would all seldom hang out and got along great. I would ride with her to pick him up here and there. He was a quiet, mellow guy. They were having some issues like any other young couple. At that time, I was not dating anyone and was quite okay with it. I enjoyed some days just sitting on the balcony chilling and getting to spend time with myself.

O n a whim, Sha and I came up with the idea of having a small get-together at my apartment, so we wrote a list of items we needed and the people who we were inviting. I decided to go the store while she cleaned up. While I was out, I ran into an old classmate Pete, and his friend Kevin. We had small talk and I invited them over for our gathering later that night.

On the way back home, I was thinking what kind of guy Kevin was and whether he would be good for Sha. I knew he was her type. Upon my return home, Sha proceeded to tell me who she invited, and I was blown away. I said, "Girl are you crazy? We can't fit all these people in this one-bedroom apartment." Mind you, I hardly knew anybody but Sha. On the other hand, she knew a sea of people. She was an extremely sociable person. I found out, as she rolled on the floor laughing, that she'd invited over fifty to sixty people to a *one-bedroom* apartment!!!! "Sha are you kidding me?" I asked, "How are all these people supposed to fit in here?" She laughed uncontrollably; she wasn't concerned about it at all.

As the evening progressed and the time for guests to arrive came, I happened to slip in the news to Sha about my classmate Pete and Kevin coming by and that I wanted to introduce Kevin to her. I'm usually not the matchmaking type of person; that stuff can sometimes cause more trouble than good. Sha was strongly against meeting someone blind, and to be honest, I would've been too. But for some weird reason I was insistent about it. While in the midst of trying to convince her, the doorbell rang; it was Pete and Kevin arriving as our first guests!

As I answered, Sha flew to the bedroom and shut the door. I was laughing hysterically in my mind as I invited them in. They were kind enough to bring some drinks and snacks. I extended a little hospitality, then headed to the kitchen with the items. I quickly rushed to the bedroom to tell Sha how handsome Kevin is and that she needed to get her butt out there to say hello. I told her, "I promise he's your type appearance-wise. Not sure of his personality and all that." She finally came out to meet them. When Kevin and Sha locked eyes it was like 4th of July fireworks! Sha played it cool, but I knew her, and I could tell she was about to pop. She asked the fellas to excuse us for a moment as we entered the bedroom a second time.

She shut the door and we were both gasping for air. I was excited for her and she was so excited that had I convinced her to at least meet him. We gathered ourselves accordingly and reentered the room. The doorbell began to ring off the hook… it was still early evening and we already had half the room full.

The music was pumped, conversations saturated the room, dance competitions broke out, drinks were being poured and we had major fun. Guests were still arriving in groups. It was approaching one a.m. and the get-together had evolved into a full-fledge party. As I maneuvered throughout the crowd, I witnessed Kevin and Sha were hitting it off. They hung out all during the entire party. Unaware, Kevin was known for dancing, and boy could he dance. He charged through the crowd with all his dance moves and demanded the crowd's attention. Between him and Sha, they turned it out and it was all the way live.

The intensity of the party caused us to open the doors to the balcony. The air conditioning was at its limit and it was still smokey in there. The bell rang late evening and it was the police asking who's place it was and I said, "It's my place, sir." He said there were complaints of the music being too loud. I apologized to the officers and said I would comply. The officers were pretty cool; they said they understood it was a clean party and warned us to keep it down. I then asked them what time they get off and that they were welcome to come by. Surprisingly, one of the officers came back and partied a bit with us and we all had a blast. Never had that happened before, but it was cool.

Around early morning guests began to dwindle down. Kevin and Sha were still in deep conversation, but Pete was ready to retire for the evening. Kevin and Sha exchanged contact information and they left. We were exhausted and left everything where it was. We cleaned up the next day.

Sha and I recovered from the prior evening and our friendship was tighter than it'd ever been. We always had each other's back. A short time span had gone by and things were going well with Sha and I until this evening, one unpredicted, horrible night in which I never want to experience again. Ever!

I was home alone, chilling, having an extremely vulnerable moment in my singleness and was really trying to work through it. It was raining profusely and suddenly my doorbell began to ring repeatedly. The few people who know me know I don't open doors unless I'm aware of your arrival or I really know you. I asked who it was, and it was Sha's boyfriend. I was wondering, why is he here? Sha hadn't said anything to me about him coming by. I opened the door because he sounded as if it was urgent. As I let him in, he proceeded to tell me that he had a flat tire in the area, and he needed to use the phone. I said sure and went to the rest room thinking nothing of it. I assumed he was calling Sha because I was going to call her just to let her know he was at my place.

Before that could occur, as I was coming from the ladies' room I was surprisingly gripped around my waist and sort of pulled from the tiny hallway to my bedroom and was seductively shoved on my bed by my best friend's boyfriend. As he strongly came on to me, I was still trying to gather my thoughts while at the same time telling him he needs to leave. I was desperately trying not to succumb to my own vulnerabilities as I had in the past, and it worked temporarily. Though we engaged, we didn't go all the way because I gathered enough inner strength and authority to tell him I'm going to tell Sha and demanded that he leave immediately. He then retreated, lifted himself off me, but then threatened me that he was planning to tell Sha his version of what happened. He then had the nerve to ask me, "Who do you think she will believe?"

I felt my heart sink into a deep, dark hole of despair, feeling like the betrayer and not knowing what to do. I had never been in a situation like that in my life and became instantly conflicted. I knew I should tell her, but fear held me hostage; being torn between her not believing me and the gripping fear of losing my friend altogether if I told her and she didn't believe me.

I allowed the tormenting thoughts of blackmail to not allow me courage enough to tell my best friend; so, I never did. I was mentally held hostage by the darkness and paralysis of fear! A big mistake! Not telling her gave the enemy more ammunition to the shame and guilt.

A long lapse of time had gone by and one day it was revealed. She was told by her boyfriend and she confronted me with it. I told her yes it had happened. I was attempting tell her that it didn't happen all the way and that he came to me unannounced; but, at that point she didn't even want to hear what I was saying. She was, understandably heartbroken, hurt, and angry all at once.

She and her family were disappointed and saddened, and Sha was no longer interested in our friendship. I took this extremely hard once I was able to reflect on what had happened. The boyfriend knew that Sha was becoming disinterested in him and was drifting away, and he had used me as a pawn with the hopes that she would run back to him. I was traumatized with being a betrayer by not exposing the truth to her first, as well as being betrayed and set up; guilty and angry all at once.

To be clear, this was not a rape, but an encounter in which I was blindsided during one of my intense vulnerable moments and unexpectedly found myself seduced by the trap of the enemy. This was a whole set up. The enemy had to create confusion and distort the whole relationship to keep me in the web of rejection, one of the stronghold spirits I've fought my entire life.

From that time forth, many years went by with me holding the grief of losing my best friend in my heart. There was not a day I didn't miss her. I missed us. The deep pain of loss led to falling on my knees in prayer calling on the name of the Lord, asking Him to take the rejection and pain of grief away. I gave my life back to him and in my personal study on repentance and forgiveness, He led me to the passage of scripture where it states, "If you have wronged someone in anyway, get up from prayer and go to your brother or sister and get it right with them; ask for their forgiveness". I asked the Lord, "What if she doesn't forgive me?" He clearly said, "that part is my job, just be obedient and I will take care of the rest."

A few days went by, and I gathered the courage to step out on faith and called, trembling as the phone rang, fearing rejection. She answered the phone. I proceeded to tell her who I was and asked her how she and the family was doing. Her response was extremely dry and seemingly uninterested. I told her the nature of my call, asked her to forgive me she responded with, "Okay" and the called ended.

I wept profusely after that call; it was like a release off my spirit.

Months later I was exercising and briskly walk as I had been doing for months, headed down a long strip of walkway, when I saw a car make a sudden U-turn. I didn't pay much attention to it. The car started to slow down. I assumed it was some man trying to "holla". To my surprise, I heard a baby-like voice that sounded much like Sha's. She called my name and I just about lost it. Tears began to well up in me. She pulled over and we embraced with a tight hug. She said she saw me walking and said if she can forgive her ex-boyfriend, she could forgive me too. God instantly remined me that His Word did not return to Him void...He said, "See, I didn't forget. I'm a keeper of my word." That day was a profound moment and I cried tears of joy. Not only because I had witnessed, for the first time in my life, what the power of Godly reconciliation looked like, to actually know that God heard and moved on my behalf.

All I can say is, obedience is always better than sacrifice. The faithfulness of God's promises, if we would only trust and take Him at His word. There is power in forgiveness. Forgiveness breeds wholeness and healing.

Guess what? What the devil meant for evil, God turned and designed it for good. Kevin and Sha had really hit it off. They later married and had a son while we were estranged. I was ecstatic to hear that, but tragically found out Kevin was killed in a car accident shortly after they married. Sha raised an amazing son, in whom I'm proud to call nephew. God has restored and redeemed them from it all. We are more connected as family now than we were before. To God be all the glory!!!!!!

**Trap Three**

Going about my business as usual, I headed to the laundromat. Upon arrival, I did what all others do: walk back and forth getting my baskets of laundry out of the car and proceed to set up and get change. I think I had filled about two to three washers and had started to fold the first basket of clothes when I noticed a man staring at me in my peripheral vision. I kind of looked up and he made eye contact with me, slightly smiling. I said to myself, "I know he's not smirking at me. Maybe he's just looking in my direction." I looked over my shoulder to see who he could be smiling at but there was no one behind me. I then realized I was his focus. Well I continued to mind my own business with the thought, "I just want to get this laundry done and get on with it." I was in a point in my life where I was in my early to mid-twenties, and I was flustered with my prior relationships, feeling alone and vulnerable inwardly, and was just over the repeated cycle kind of bad relationships. I had made some progress in my healing, but not enough to be in a relationship.

However, since I would never give him total eye contact, he proceeded to approach me from across the room. My first thought was, "Here we go! "Why does this always happen when I'm minding my own business?" He introduced himself and asked me if that was my first time there. I told him. "yes'. I liked that the laundry facility was extremely nice and upscale; big screen TVs, brand new washers and dryers, a small eating area, etc. It was a typical laundromat. I then ask him how long he had been managing the place and his response was, "I'm not the manager. I'm the owner."

I was stunned. I didn't believe him, so he took me over to a wall where he hung his credentials and showed me his name, Al W., and his driver's license. Reflecting on the fact that he was much older, I was slightly impressed. He was very laid-back; ambitious and was pursuing other business endeavors. The content of our conversation intrigued me.

When it came to business, Al had a brilliant mind, but when it came to outward appearance, Lord have mercy! He needed help! He was stuck in the seventy's. He was in his mid to late thirties. His hair was long, silky, somewhat semi-wavy and he sported a ponytail with a red collard green rubber band; might I add he wore an earring. He was attractive, but way behind time in the fashion world. Normally this would have turned me completely off, but I had matured a little and somehow the long list of deal breakers to help gauge me in relationships had grown smaller.

I finished washing and folding while having off-and-on conversations with Al. I had gathered my baskets of clothes and items and headed toward the door when he hastily met me at the entrance and insisted that he take my things to the car. I was quite appreciative and thanked him as I entered my vehicle. He asked me when I would be returning and I replied, "I will probably be back next week." He responded with a smile on his face and said, "Please do, I'll be looking forward to it. I would like to get to know you." I just smiled and drove off. To be candid, I was flattered a little, but not enough to give myself permission to be overwhelmed by his little gesture of kindness. As the weeks went by, I visited every week for the course of a few months, and each visit, our conversations became more intense.

We eventually got to know each other enough where he obviously felt comfortable enough to ask me to dinner and to spend some quality time with me. I was quite hesitant at first, but I had never dated an older man and was totally unfamiliar with mature conversation and having someone to show interest in me and my views. My suspicion raised questions like: Why me? What's in it for you? Why are you taking time with me?

His reply was, "Why not?" He went on to say how mature I was in holding diverse conversation and not being overly impressed with him. He was intrigued, and it cause him to want to know me better; age wasn't a concern for him. I had always been mature, in some areas, for my age but had never dated anyone who would appreciate it. I told him to let me think about it and I would keep him informed.

After a few weeks of me not responding to his invitation, his persistence intensified. I eventually conceded and agreed to meet him at his place, which wasn't far from his business. This was somewhat uncomfortable because this was never something I did for a first date but reluctantly made the decision to cross my own boundary.

He arranged everything and asked that I meet him after he closed at the laundromat. I agreed, looking forward to a simple dinner and conversation. I arrived at the laundromat, waited in the car and he beckoned for me to come in. Thinking that he had to finish up some business before we left for his place to have dinner, I was shocked when I found out we were at his place — in the back of the laundromat!

It was very classy, with a sports bar feel, but nevertheless... it was still a laundromat. When entering the back of the business, there was a whole entire lounge area, kind of "plushed out"; it was like being in a cozy and intimate jazz spot. He had obviously been living there for a minute. Everything was in its place. As he turned the volume up on the jazz and we began to engage in conversation I felt my defenses dwindle. After a while I was so tuned into him, I forgot we were in the back of a laundromat.

A few dates in this atmosphere and him conveying to me that he was really into me, it wasn't long before I found myself "turnt up" in the bed of sin with Al. I was then bound in a soul tie that only God could deliver me from.

We routinely met up every week until he relocated to his apartment. I'd become comfortable with this arrangement, being led only by how I felt when Al treated me like I mattered and would offer to assist me in whatever I needed. Even though my relationship with God was shaky, I knew this was wrong, but my feelings superseded my Godly conviction. I justified it in my own head and accepted it all. I just couldn't get the strength to move on.

I continued to see Al; we operated as a secret couple in my eyes. We never traveled further than the corner store, and I would insist on one of us staying in the car. My best friend at the time wanted to know who this guy was I was spending so much time with. I usually shared pretty much everything with her, but not this time. I kept it from everyone, including her, until one day Al insisted on picking me up while I lived with my best friend and her family. That's when she realized I was going out with an older man. She really didn't agree with it but warned me to be careful.

One evening, we planned to have dinner, play cards, watch a couple of flicks and chill. As I approached his door, I heard the beautiful sound of jazz playing. I absolutely love jazz. As I was about to ring the doorbell, he opened the door with anxious expectation. He ushered me to his seating area while offering me a beverage as dinner was almost ready. I can't recall if he prepared dinner or had it ordered, but nonetheless, it smelled amazing. We engaged in small talk until dinner was ready. We ate, conversed, and had more conversation about life, his daughter, investments, how money works, etc. Al was very intellectual and full of business knowledge. He shared some of his aspirations and dreams of owning diverse businesses and strategies on how to pay a home off in full. He not only owned the laundry mat; he was on the brink of opening a hair salon and office building office suites. This was so refreshing, and I appreciated the focus of the conversation as he shared the blueprints and business plans for his future.

After that night, we had many other quiet evenings at his place and to be quite honest, he would offer to take me out to various places, but I wouldn't agree. I didn't want to be embarrassed being seen with him and risk running into someone I knew. I didn't want to explain why I was with a man way older than myself. When I tell you "Poly" and "Ester" (polyester) were his best friends! The man couldn't dress to save his life. I mean that's all he knew, shake and wear, no ironing necessary! I didn't want to be seen in public with him dressed like that. Even though he was older, he had a some-what youthful look. Inwardly, I felt kind of bad but I no idea how to tell him he was about three decades behind in the way he dressed.

That was so selfish of me. All I was thinking about at the time was me and my image. He was used to dating women who never cared about him nor his fashion sense. They were only concerned about what they could gain financially. Fashion wasn't his focus, obviously, but vision was. He was a decent man who was just stuck in the 70's. The friendship was going well, and I would often think about how different this was for me, as I had only previously dated younger or immature dudes. They were often impatient, uncaring, quick to get in your "drawers" and just never seemed to have a desire to get to know me as a person. I would always attract those types of dudes and never could figure out why, so to me what I had with Al was heading in a good direction.

Well, during one of my normal visits with him, I had drunk a few glasses of wine and had to make a restroom run. We agreed to watch a movie. However, I came out of the rest room and there was straight up porn on the screen. It totally stunned me. As I stuttered, I abruptly said to him, "That is not a movie, what are you doing?" He responded with the softest and non-threatening tone, "Why are you upset? It's okay." Now just to be clear, from my memory bank I didn't recall ever watching any porn or nothing related to it, so this was way out of my league. Even though something in me knew this too wasn't right for me, I continued to give my ear to Al's soft and cunning words as I allowed strong lustful sounds and scenes on the television. I felt something rise in me and it felt like an out-of-body experience. Like someone had injected me with a heavy dose of "liquid lust". The feeling was almost immobilizing but strongly intoxicating.

I was disappointed in Al for putting me in such an awkward scenario, however, I found my "like/love" feelings for him to, again override what I knew wasn't good for me. Al was never demanding or controlling, and I guess that was what was confusing. To be candid, even though I was angry with him in the moment, I was also focused more on how he made me feel than what was real, and this is the very bait Satan cast out for me to consume and I succumbed to doing just that.

Before I could fully comprehend, I was hooked, caught, and eventually trapped simultaneously, in my emotional need to be needed, loved, and appreciated. And this was the very cocktail the enemy used to open me up to the "spirit of perversion".

How many of us, especially us ladies, dumb down our standards and overlook obvious red flag warnings due to desperation of just not wanting to be alone, hoping he chooses you to be a keeper? We walk into these unhealthy, "situationships" with what I call "open-shut eyes". You do know the longer we linger in places we shouldn't be in, the tighter and deeper the trap becomes, and nobody can get you out but God. Yep! Even though I knew I should have been more direct and stuck to how I felt concerning porn, the bond strengthened as we were now bound together by another level of sexual and emotional soul ties!!! From fornication to porn. That appetite was alive and always hungry for its next fix!

The more sex, no intimacy, we engaged in, the more it became my new norm. I had become so comfortable with watching porn with him it was like eating popcorn during your favorite flick. He was still kind and thoughtful, but porn had him and he had introduced it to me. I wasn't addicted and would only watch it when I was with him because that's what he wanted. My fear was if I really told him how I felt, I would no longer be wanted. I was still dealing with the fear of being rejected and abandoned.

Fear, abandonment, rejection, and identity issues are all components that draw you into traps that can bound you to toxic and repetitive cycles you can't escape on your own. You do know, by the cunning and crafty skill of the devil, that traps can be disguised and/or wrapped in packages that seem of no threat? For example, "well he's a businessman", "owns his own home", "I feel safe with him", loves his mom, etc. were *all* traps.

Traps don't have to look deceptive to be deceptive, and this is a subtle tactic the enemy uses to draw you right in his territory with the intent to keep you bound for seasons of your life, sucking time away from your true destiny you can never get back.

## The Trap Deepens

I had arrived at Al's for another planned laid-back evening. When I approached the door, I heard jazz playing as usual but this time I also heard a woman's voice, so I rang the bell. He didn't answer. I rang again and again, and he never came to the door, so I left. I was upset and knew that the relationship had taken a shift! As I headed back home, I was" like, "What in the Sam Hill is going on?"

The next day he called to explain. I was livid but needed to hear his response. He gave it to me straight and revealed to me that he was married! What! Married?

I couldn't believe it. The triggers of rejection began to boil up and I went into a fury panic. The voice I had heard was his wife who had dropped by unannounced. To avoid confrontation, he chose not to come to the door. Al went on to say they had been separated for many months and were at the last phase of their divorce. I expressed to him that I don't do separated men, and he needed to close that door before there was a future anything.

Entangled now in a trio of mess, not only was I in fornication, and perversion(porn), I was now in a whole soul-tie with adultery! With that being said, I pulled all the way out. That was the dealbreaker.

I endured the withdrawals of the relationship, with the intent in mind that this was the end. We departed and didn't see each other for months. No communication with Al at all. I took a small break, disappointed in myself and sick of myself all at once. I pleaded with God asking him:

"Why am I not worthy of being happy?

Why can't I get this right?

"Please help me out of this habitual cycle!"

Months later, after having to detox my soul and spirit from it all, God laid the cards on the table. He confirmed to me that He was my heavenly Father and He made me and viewed me in His image. He went on to tell me that there was nothing I could do to make Him retrack His love and the plans He had for me; and how I didn't see me from His lens, but only my unworthy, unclean, rejected lens. When God really shows you yourself, it will totally liberate your life to His freedom. He saved me, delivered me, and set me free in areas I thought I would never break away from such as the stronghold of fornication and cycles of emotional and mental trauma that kept me bound!

Many months later, Al and I crossed paths again. We were both in better places in our lives. I felt cleaner, lighter, and freer than I had ever been. The cleansing of God is such a powerful necessity. He shared how he really loved me, he no longer was a part of his sin cycle and that He had given his life to the Lord. He proceeded to say how much I had impacted his life. He had been checking up on me without my knowledge and heard how my life had really changed and how much I was pouring into others. He was truly remorseful, repented to God and asked for my forgiveness for everything he possibly could have done that wasn't profitable to my life. I accepted his apology and expressed to him how happy I was for him and hoped that his life continued to see and feel the God's glory upon it. We talked frequently but this time we started out fresh, no boo thang, no sex, no putting myself in the wrong positions. He respected my boundaries and was quite intrigued by it. He had never been challenged like this before in all his life. I could tell Al's relationship with God was rather new but committed.

Al had relocated to Jersey and started two businesses and would come in and out of Atlanta quite frequently to see his daughter. We ignited, yes, another relationship but this time it was cultivated a whole new way.

In the meantime, I was still struggling with his attire situation and now he wanted to meet my friends and accountability circle. I didn't know what to do! I laughed out loud! Al a romantic and loved to show up unexpectedly with gifts and surprises. So true story, Al knew that when he planned to visit Atlanta, he had to let me know in advance so that I could schedule my hair clients accordingly. I was still working at the salon with Dea and the owners of the salon. We had become a tight knit family and they held me accountable for my personal and business life.

As I was working in the salon one Friday it was packed with everyone's client wall-to-wall, including mine. We were in the groove, getting clients in and out, listening to CeCe Winans and Kirk Franklin's "Stomp" (Can you tell I remember this like yesterday? *laugh out loud* I was at the back-shampoo bowl encouraging one of my clients when I got a buzz on the phone from Jay, the owner. He was always stationed up front to guard the door as he worked. Jay announced to me that "Poly and Esther" were there to see me. I had an expression on my face like who is that? I had no idea who "Poly and Esther" was. I come around the corner to greet them and to my embarrassing surprise, it was Al. He had just come in town and he was determined to meet my circle, so he came with roses and gifts and dinner plans.

He showed up wearing a polyester pant suit with his long hair bound in a ponytail with a red collard green rubber band. Yes, he was still dressing the exact same way. I was so embarrassed, and Jay, Dea and Viv were screaming as I tried to play it cool and had no choice but to introduce him. He was a sweet guy but when I tell you that scene was like when" Huggie Bear" got out of jail on the movie *I'm Gonna Get You Sucka!* He thought he still had it going on and had walked out of jail stuck in the last two decades.

I tried to usher Al out of there as fast as I could by convincing him that I had too many people to chat and that I would see him later for dinner. As I walked back to my station the jokes came flooding in. It was the joke for what seemed like the rest of the year! We all laughed every day for weeks! It was ridiculously comical. In the back of my mind I was constantly asking God, "What is this?" and "Is this your will?"?

One day, I received a phone call from Al while he was still in Jersey. He sounded upset. He then laid one on me. He shared with me that after our breakup, that his now ex-wife, called him and told him that he probably needed to go to the doctor. He asked why and she revealed to him that she had an STD; he probably had it too! I asked, "Why are you telling me this?" And "Are you alright?" Initially, I wasn't worried at all because I knew I had been abstinent for quite some time. He answered with hesitation and replied with a "No." He went on to say that his ex-wife deliberately concealed this news until after they had divorced out of bitterness and revenge.

My heart began to flutter, and major anxiety kicked in with, "Oh my God, do I have it?

"We were together then"

"Is she lying?"

I panicked, saying to myself, "God, I've been fervently praying for you to cleanse me from all unrighteousness. You delivered me from fornication… I was withholding preparing myself for marriage" Why this? Why now?

Al caught a flight and met up with me in Atlanta. I was at a loss for words. Al looked me straight in the eyes and asked me to marry him, holding a large "diamonded-up" ring! To add to my emotions, this charged my mind with more questions.

"Should I?"

"What if I don't?"

"If I don't', then who else is going to marry me with a STD?"

"Am I sure this is what God wants for me?"

I responded by asking him to give me some time. This was a lot in a span of a few moments. I had to know that this was the will of God. I didn't go through hell and high water to wait and then say "yes" to the wrong one, even if he was good to me.

I remembered learning that in the multitude of counsel there is safety. My emotions were calm, and the Holy Spirit reminded me that I had just had a physical two weeks before and there were no signs of anything. I had a clean bill of health. I was still worried a little and the Holy Spirit said, "Whatever you asked in my name, according to the will of God, He will grant it."

I fasted and prayed and sought godly counsel from Dea and Jay, while trusting for wisdom and an overwhelming peace and calm in my spirit. Dea asked me the hard questions, but they were necessary. She asked,

"Are you really ready to handle this STD situation if you marry him?"

"Is this just your infatuation with what you wanted it to be?"

"Do you really love him?"

I was hesitant. She said that may be my answer.

Dea was a straight-shooter and never watered anything down! When she asked if I loved him a bell went off in my head. I knew in my spirit, but it wasn't God's best for me.

I turned him down. He was utterly devasted, but I had to obey God. I realized that this man really loved me, but the feeling wasn't mutual. I broke it off and cut all ties so that he could heal and move on with his life.

The moral of this segment is the awesome grace of God! I cried for days afterwards because there was no way I shouldn't have contracted that STD! I knew what I had done, and the overwhelming revelation of God's mercy and grace still grips me to this day. God had more for me, and He commanded the death angel to pass me by. God confirmed to me later that He had plans for me, plans to prosper me, and bring me to an expected end! He covered me while I was still in my sin and I know that I was, and I am justified by faith!!! His undeserving gift has given me life.

**Trap Four**

It was the middle of the day as I headed over to the mall to take a small lunch break and run a few errands while I had clients under the hair dryer (the days of roller sets under the hot dryer). I made it back to my car when I heard, "Excuse me! May I ask what's your name?" As I turned around, I was surprised to see this handsome guy with curly hair and a countenance of confidence. I asked him if he was talking to me because there were several women in my proximity. He replied, "Yes. You."

I replied with my name and he proceeded to tell me his name was Kris; he had been admiring me from afar. I said, "Nice to meet you," and proceeded to walk off in a haste to get back to my clients. He caught up with me asked me for my number and I told him I don't give my number out to people I don't know but I would take his instead. He reluctantly agreed and I headed back to work. Couple of weeks passed and I did call him up. He was surprised that I called and to be honest, I was too.

Over the next few months, our conversations became frequent. During this time in my life, I was struggling with my relationship with God and I was straddling the fence, vacillating between two paths: my way or God's. As we became really acquainted with one another, I learned Kris was a really great singer. His voice was a soulful, bluesy mix. He told me he worked for some big company and his home state was Michigan. We hung out, dined, listened to music, had great conversations. Things seemed pretty cool.

They both were straight shooters. I ran this dude Kris by my accountability partners, Dea and Jay. They reminded me of who I belonged to and encouraged me to seek the Lord out and don't be moved by my emotions. They had no opinion nor objective at the time but oh, they were watching.

Not long after, I'd become pretty acquainted with Kris and in this space, unaware my guards were no longer a priority. Disappointedly, I found myself engaged in sensual conversations that led to sex. I fought it but once that fire is lit, it's hard to shut it down. Fornication was a serious stronghold in my life and trying to fight it in my own strength always led to failure every single time. Shame and guilt flooded my conscious and I just wanted to hide. My consistent prayer was asking God to please help me break this and no longer swing in and out of His will.

Almost immediately after giving up my "goods", the relationship shifted. We had been together for about a year and a half. We had so many conversations about marriage but there was this subtle doubt in my gut and I just couldn't put my hand on it.

Fast forward a bit, Kris pops the question "Will you marry me?"

Shocked and confused, torn between my heart's desire to marry and fear of missing what I thought was my only chance, I reluctantly said "Yes." But here's the kicker— he had no ring and suggested that I purchase a ring on my credit, and he would reimburse me for it. Like the ultimate dummy, I did it! Boy, we as women can make some dumb decisions under the influence of desperation!

After the proposal, Kris became distracted. When we were together it seemed like his mind was somewhere else. The pattern of cancelled dates, sporadic unanswered calls, etc. When I confronted him about it, he agitatedly confessed that he had lost his job; the job I still really didn't know much about. His place was laid, and he was very meticulous about everything. His apartment was filled with colorful art pieces and paintings. So, I took it for what he said and to me that kind of explained why he was in such a funk. Kris didn't handle pressure well, so I consoled him through in the effort to support.

In the meantime, I go to work one day and Dea hits me with some news that the Lord was calling her back home to Tennessee; her parents were getting older and she needed to be near them. I was greatly disappointed, but I totally understood. My accountability partner was moving, and I had all kinds of anxiety about it. Dealing with my mother's controlling spirit, Dea would be the one who could talk me off the ledge.

Consumed with an abundance of conflicting thoughts my spirit was heavy. Pushing thru a busy workday at the salon, Dea, being who she is, asked me "What's wrong with you?" Dea was one of the few people I had shared the news of my engagement with and she looked at me and said, "For someone who's getting married, you sure don't act like it; you ain't smiling and you ain't telling nobody, so what's up?." I didn't want to admit how embarrassed I was about the proposal, the lack of a ring, and my apprehension. Dea knew that this wasn't what God wanted for me, but she didn't push the envelope. I knew she was interceding for me because I didn't have any peace about this situation at all, but I continued submitting myself to it for the sake of feeling like a failure once again.

Not long after, Dea relocated. I almost made the decision to relocate with her. I wavered between giving up my clientele and starting all over. This seemed to be the perfect opportunity to get away from being under my mom's control. I really needed a change of scenery, however I decided to stay in Georgia. But you better believe every chance I got I was on the road to Tennessee. I was there so much it became a second home.

Kris' attitude towards Dea and Jay grew worst as time progressed. In fact, anyone who was influential in my life wasn't his cup of tea. Dea eventually told me before she left, "You need to keep ya eyes open!" I took it with a grain of salt, thinking he was just going through a rough patch and needed support.

Well, the plot came to an aggressive simmer. I got a call from Kris telling me that he was moving immediately. "What do you mean you're moving?" I asked. "How and why and what about all your furniture and stuff?" He said he had sold it all. He was moving to Tennessee. Apparently, he had landed a job there; in the same city where Dea now lived. I found that crazy and ironic at the same time. Mind you, he never told me what job it was or where he was living. With an urgent sound in his voice he promised to call me when he got settled and quickly hung up. I looked at the phone in disbelief!

I didn't hear from Kris for weeks; until I got a call from him on a pay phone. He claimed that he was excited about landing a job and finding a place to live at the top of the mountain in Tennessee. I was shocked that he was living on a mountain, but he insisted that was the only place he could find.

As you may know, a long-distance relationship can be challenging especially when there's already suspicions of infidelity. Now that Jay and Dea lived in Tennessee too, I had even more reason to visit my fiancé and my peeps concurrently. Our relationship had been shaky, and we had been in strong disagreement mode constantly. The intensity of our relationship had become like swimming against a tide.

I brought the matter to God. However, the more I read, the more I felt convicted. Holy Spirit said, "Cut off the sex and you will really see what your relationship is built on!" That thing resonated in my spirit and I decided to try and see if it worked. I needed to do it for myself. I had the backing of Jay and Dea by way of prayer.

After asking for the strength to stand on my decision, I had the conversation with Kris and the backlash from hell came with a vengeance.

# Chapter 13

## The Plot Thickens

O ne day, I planned a surprise visit to see Kris. I wanted us to have dinner and really try to work on our relationship; see if we could move forward. I called Dea up to let her know I was coming and needed to stay at her place for accountability.

I arrived and went straight to Dea's salon to pick up the key so I could drop my things off at her house and come back to the salon.

I called Kris from the salon to surprise him. I could hear the shock and hesitation in his voice. When I got to him, he wanted to know why I was there. We embraced, exchanged cars, and made plans to have dinner after work to talk things out. I drove back to the salon.

Thirty minutes or so I heard an announcement about a grey Audi blocking a client from leaving. That was me — in Kris' car. As I walked towards the car, I saw a yellow sticky note on the window saying, "I've been calling you and paging you. Where are you and when are you coming home?" Surprisingly, I played it cool, but I was fuming!

I had been played like a straight up fool! I folded the note, placed it in my pocket and headed to pick him up. As Kris hopped in the car with excitement, he smacked me on the lips and asked, "What's up?" I responded calmly but inside I really wanted to rip him to shreds.

We drove to his place so he could dress for dinner, halfway up the windy mountain. We arrived at the spaceship looking contraption he was renting. He attempted to seduce me, but I intercepted by handing him the note, followed by," Who is this?" As I expected, at first, he denied it and then confessed to being with someone else the entire time we were together. I was relieved even though my heart was aching. I immediately made the decision to walk away from that two-year relationship.

I called Dea while bawling! Surprisingly, the Holy Spirit had already revealed it to her.

Once I got to her, she looked at me with a smile and revealed that the very same thing had happened to her around that time in her life. She assured me that this was not the end of my life but the birthing of something new.

### God's "No" Will Save Your Life

During my meditation, one morning I asked God, "Why didn't it work out with Kris?

A few weeks later, God answered my question. I found out that Kris had left Atlanta because he was running from trouble. Our entire relationship had been a lie from the beginning. Kris and his girlfriend were engaged in illegal dealings; the apartment wasn't his but his secret girlfriend. She was an airline stewardess and had been transporting illegal weapons on the plane. Law Enforcement had been in hot pursuit to apprehend them and everyone connected to them. Kris had to hightail it out of the state and hide. It hit me, "Oh my God! Lord you were protecting me the entire time! That is why I never had peace about marrying him!"

That day is when I learned God's "no" is His divine protection as a Father. Rejection teaches us to receive a lie and deny truth in fear of not having the desires of your heart. He will allow some things to fall apart for His will to be done. I had a revelation while sitting there in my car and thinking about all the times I was in that apartment. I could have been arrested in their illegal mess and gone to prison for something I had nothing to do with. I had been totally unaware.

So many women and girls get caught up this way every day and end up being sentenced to long prison time for something they were totally oblivious of. That day, for the first time, I recognized God's love for me. I was encouraged to press on like never before and live the life God planned for me.

Every trap had been strategically set to keep me entangled in deceptive cycles of thinking and believing the lies of the enemy. The weapons were formed but they did not prosper. God's grace was sufficient in it all.

# Chapter 14

## A Divine Setup

I landed a job working at a credit card company. When I arrived for the interview there was an attractive dark-chocolate-complexion young lady sitting at the receptionist desk. She was instructing people on where to go and what to do upon arrival.

Fortunately, I was hired, and Carla and I hit it off at the workplace. She was an incredibly attractive and feisty young lady yet comical. Our workplace relationship evolved into a personal one. I eventually met her family, hung out and really bonded with them.

One day, we were standing in her yard when this beautiful shiny Cutlass car pulled up. A handsome, chocolate, bow legged man got of the car and started shooting the breeze with Carla. I thought he was just some guy she was interested in because they seemed to be so comfortable with each other. He eventually asked her who I was, and she finally introduced us. He smiled as he spoke to me and she introduced him as her old cousin, "Blacky". I then excused myself and didn't think much more about it.

Once she came back into house, Carla told me that her cousin's name was Lamar. She gave me the run down on how cool he was and how he took great care of his son.

Carla and I became inseparable and eventually I was invited to live with her. I accepted. I was still being plagued by my mom's controlling spirit and I refused to go home so I stayed wherever God graced me. I had no idea her parents were ministers until after I moved in. I said, "God, no you didn't set me up like this to live with a preacher, knowing what I'd suffered from being a PK (preacher's kid)!"

Her father was extremely comical and loved to tell stories while he snacked. The more I listened to him the more I realized he had a different perspective than my dad's as a preacher. He didn't believe in shoving the Bible down your throat. I honestly believe God placed me there for more reasons than I could comprehend.

Lamar and I became really tight. He really was a good guy who unfortunately was caught up in that street life but didn't know how to get out. He started coming around so often, that one day Carla's father blurted out of the blue. "Lamar, you going to marry that girl one day!" Shocked was an understatement! However, Lamar just looked and smiled. Carla started laughing so hard; she was cracking up over the look on my face. I brushed that off quick and moved on to something else.

A year later, Carla had this idea of us moving into our own place as roomies. I wasn't too sure about the idea but intrigued. We decided to take the leap and moved around the corner from her parents. Lamar and I developed a pretty special friendship.

Carla and I, on a whim, planned to have a small house party with a few people. However, this small house party quickly escalated to a block party with the street jammed packed with cars. Of course, Lamar came through, well-groomed as usual.

I really wasn't into the party as much as I was interested in talking with him about the lifestyle thing again. He finally told me that I was right; he really was tired of looking over his shoulder, dodging the 'po-po', and was sick of all the begging women, etc. He in turn asked me, "Why haven't you asked me for anything? I told him I didn't need anything from him, just his friendship. He had enough people to take care of between family and the beggars, so I was good. He said, "I know you're a good girl and I do know this lifestyle is not for me anymore. I just have to figure a way out of this." He then added that he would love for us to be more than friends, but at the time he knew his lifestyle wasn't good for me. He told me to go on and live my life and do what I knew I should do. That night he pretty much bided me farewell.

He really didn't come around much after that. It was his way of protecting me and I respected him for that. My prayer for him was "Lord deliver him out of these streets. Protect him!"

That night, after pondering over my entire life, I decided to stop running from God for the last time. It was past time for change.

Carla had no idea what was taking place in my heart but my desire for frivolous living had come to an end. When I made that decision, the voice of God resounded so strong, it was almost scary.

Despite that God-encounter, I still tried to date one of my past flings. But the final straw didn't come until one night when I'd invited a man over and while in the very act, I heard the voice of God so loudly saying, "Stop it now!" I heard it three times. I ran out of that house — half- dressed, bra half on, jumped in my car and drove down the street. I needed to get out. And then I remembered — that was my house!

I turned around, drove back to my house, and told that guy that he had to leave immediately. I gave him no explanation. I didn't even know how to explain it if I'd tried. I felt as if I was literally consuming my own vomit. Going back to old cycles and flings, only serves to reinforce bondages and leaves you with another layer of false security.

God was dealing with me strongly. The next morning, I made the decision to tell Carla that I was leaving but I would give her enough time to find another roommate. I had to go.

Later that day I called my grandmother and asked her if I could stay with her; I needed some down time to get my life together. I knew that would be a place where there were the least chances of temptation. She gladly said yes.

When I moved there, I put a restriction on myself: go to work, pay my grandmother, no more dating period and find my way back to the altar of repentance. I had to starve the appetites that fed my flesh. I delved into consistently reading the word of God which strengthened my faith. I was craving for the understanding of my broken emotions and toxic cycles that had me bound

I reached out to my Dea seeking counsel. She was so happy to hear I was ready to surrender all but warned me that Satan was going to turn up the warfare in an attempt to get me trapped again. Dea shared scriptures with me about temptation and different traps and games the enemy set for people; especially when they make a genuine decision and effort to change masters. This infuriated him. Just that little information was enough to jumpstart me into waging war against the devil with the word of God. I knew what to look for. This time I wouldn't be blindsided.

During the next few years, I found a teaching church, and learned how to spend time with myself. I was learning more about me. I had no idea who I was and why I was created. I made a commitment to God that I would engage in no more sex until I got married. Now that was one of the toughest challenges I had in my walk with God. My fleshly desire of just wanting to be loved but going about it the wrong way was a beast that wasn't going down easily. Killing fleshly desires literally feels like you are dying. However, the goal was to starve everything connected to my toxic cycles to death; I had to stop feeding it by bringing it under the authority of Christ. There were countless times where strong temptation was placed right in front of me but instead of taking the bait, I chose to pull on the strength of God. He came through every time. How many know there are some things that go easily and then there are some things you will have to contend with consistently in order to be free and stay free?

I stayed hidden at my grandmother's house. Very few people knew where I was. It was a great safe haven for me to grow in my relationship with God again while cutting toxic people, things, and behavior out of my life. I was in a spiritual rehabilitation.

God showed himself faithful through my stripping process. I began to see the error of my ways. Even though the emotional trauma I went through played a large part in the direction of my life, I now had to take responsibility for my own actions and no one else's. It took lots of time, sacrifice, denying flesh, will, energy, facing some fears and relentless determination that I would not go back to the vomit of my old life and nothing would come in between God and myself. I had to understand that when walking with God the process is continual not instant, intentional not perfect.

I still made mistakes and wrong choices periodically. But when I kept my eyes and heart fixed on the Lord, He always directed my path. In my detox process I shed layers and layers of emotional pain. That's just what inner healing is — layers of deliverance. I still had many layers to uncover and growing to do, even after I gave my life back to God. It took me four long years to get back to the perfect will of God and from my backslidden cycles. It wasn't that it took God that long, some of it was me not allowing Him to have full control. That's when I found God's Word that says, "God is married to the backslider, whether He returns to Him or not." He's a good Father waiting and cheering His children to come back to Him! He leaves the ninety-nine to go after the one. God's patience is insurmountable. He loved me while I was in my bed of sin, wrecked emotions, countless feelings of unworthiness, many desperate moments of loneliness and other forms of darkness all around me.

God doesn't love conditionally like man, but unconditionally. His love for us is never-ending, even when we ignorantly or intentionally make our bed in hell. Nothing can separate us from His love. All the counterfeit lovers, flings, and everything in between, could not stand against the unfailing love of my Father. When my mother and father dropped me, forsook me, left me drowning in my own emotional pool of blood, when they could only show love for me in a limited capacity, God took me up!

Psalm 27:10-14 became my lifeline. Studying the depth of this scripture from the eyes of a broken child hidden in a woman's shell, gave me profound revelation. God had me in mind even before I was in my mother's womb. I learned that even though my father and mother forsake me, the Lord would always receive me. I meditated on, *"Teach me your ways, Lord; lead me in a straight path because of my oppressors. Don't turn me over to the desire of my foes, for false witnesses rise up against me, spouting malicious accusations. I remain confident of this one thing: I will see the goodness of the Lord in the land of the living. Wait for the Lord; be strong and take heart and wait for the Lord."*

God wishes that no man perishes. God is not a dictator nor a taskmaster waiting to rule with an iron fist but He's full of loving-kindness that we would never totally understand. This is why He's called a Good Shepherd. He chooses to be good to us even when we don't deserve it. Even when were locked into our own traumas and seem to have no way out. Even when we think we are not worthy of His amazing grace. He died for it all so that we may live and have an abundant life

# Chapter 15

# My Naomi Gave Me Life

After fighting through many months of withdrawals, negative thoughts — looking all put together outwardly, but full of broken pieces inwardly — I finally came to a place in my walk with the Lord where it I felt a ray of sunshine over the long dark clouds that had followed me my entire life. Sticking with God this time and refusing to revert to my familiar relationship cycles gave me a great sense of freedom wrapped in hope like I had never experienced. This journey taught me what, and how, the trio of condemnation, unworthiness and desperation was designed to keep me in the cycle of a mental and emotional cyclone. My journey revealed God's love for me and how it was not too late for God to use me for His glory.

One of the biggest parts of my broken spirit was the deep desperate need of a mother's love. The nurturing part of my development was never experienced from my natural mother. God revealed to me that I still needed healing in this area, but I had no way of knowing how to go about it.

Emotionally unavailable mothers (parents) can have devasting effects on a child and well into their adulthood. The painful reality of wanting to have a healthy relationship with my mother was long gone, but in my deepest emotions I still desired it. So, I remembered God's Word said ask anything in His name and it shall be given. I started to fervently ask God, why didn't my mother embrace me? Why did I have such anxiety when Mother's Day arrived? The anxiety was insurmountable. Every year I would find myself just standing in the greeting card aisle, literally having an anxiety attack, getting frustrated by every card I read saying, "You were always there." "You're the best mom ever!" "I can't imagine life without you." Those cards would frustrate me to the point I would have mini anxiety attacks right in the middle of the store. Year after year I would just robotically choose a card and maybe a cherry pie, one of her favorites, and give it to her only to feel the strong energy of rejection overtaking me as I presented my gift to her. I knew in the depth of my soul that this was not the way God intended mother and daughter relationships to be. Nonetheless the feelings were real. Over the years, every attempt of trying to connect with my mother, long into my adult years, was always rejected in some way. So, my drive to try anymore was completely depleted. Coming to grips seemed easier than trying to defend the purity of my motive.

After prayer one day, pleading with God to heal the hole in my heart from mother wounds I had since inception, I headed to work at the salon. There I met a woman who was one of the clients Dea transferred to me after she relocated back home. She said she had been watching me work with my clients and said she desired to become a continual client. We scheduled her weekly appointment and became more acquainted. It seemed so effortless to converse with her about many things. Our relationship grew close rather quickly. I've always been taught to respect my elders, but it never felt like because she was so easy to talk to and never had a problem with me asking her anything.

I've always been guarded when it came to a mother-figure in my life due to the deep unspoken trauma I encountered growing up. I craved that kind of relationship but never had the courage to trust anyone in that capacity. Not having that maternal nurturing left me intensely malnourished in that area. So, this scenario was quite awkward for me but seemed safe and fulfilling. Ms. Bailey (Ms. B) was a gentle and kind woman who was small in stature but walked heavy in wisdom.

Our salon environment never had a stale moment. It was during the time when black salons never had to go out and shop for anything because anything you can think of was available for sale. From bras to rib dinners, from makeup to leather suits, from fruit cups to pantyhose; there was never a dull moment. The atmosphere was always jovial, and the gospel music seemed to always keep everyone in a great mood. The owners' loving personalities gave many people an opportunity to sell their product.

Ms. B's visits were always uplifting. After a few months, our relationship transpired into a that safe, trusted place I've always desired. There was something about her persona that was difficult not to embrace. I felt safe enough to share parts of my life with her about my relationship with my mom. So many times, I would share my experience and people would shun me because they couldn't relate. Surprisingly, Ms. B never did.

Our relationship graduated to having lunch together quite often; laughing, talking, and sharing our personal life experiences. Our conversations were priceless, and I looked forward to her coming in for her appointment because I never knew what direction our conversations would take. Her loving voice was one that was very inviting and would make you "spill guts" even when you weren't expecting to. Ms. B loved God and her passion for women to be free from bondage illuminated through her words of correction, revelation, and encouragement. I think this was the very combination that drew me to her. Her strong mothering spirit was what I needed in spite of the intense anxiety I would feel fighting the very thing that I needed.

I became an avid reader and I was serious about desiring to please God in my single season of life. I had done it wrong for so long and this time I was determined to do it His way. My life was being processed, stripped, convicted and rebuilt by God himself and it wasn't easy breaking cycles of wrong perspectives, toxic behavior, repeated times of running back to the vomit of my past due to familiarity; not willing to allow God to empty me out and fully process me. And this is what Ms. B saw in me. She recognized that I was fighting for my life — wanting to be who God called me to be, but I still needed revelation in order to dispel the lies of the enemy in my head.

I met Ms. B when I was in the middle of my process; trying to break free from the pressure of living two lives, fleshly and spiritual. I genuinely wanted to go all out for God but did not trust Him enough to staff my life through His will for me. I insisted on helping God out by continually inviting the wrong people, mainly men, into my life. I became the narcissistic supply for anyone who were users and abusers.

After pouring out my heart to God, He spoke to me and said, "Exactly. You keep trying to create it and not trust me with it! You are not ready for the marriage I created for you because you're still married to the soul ties of your past and present. You cannot be married to Me and them. I will not share my glory with nothing and no one. I must have 1st place above all and in all. If you let me staff you with what you need to process through this season, you will experience the satisfaction of true fulfillment and joy like you've never known before."

I cried for hours because I knew I had been running from the full process of letting go and letting God lead me. Through a pool of tears and giving up trying to rush the process, God led me to the story of Naomi and Ruth. This was a phenomenal story of life after tragedy, restoration, healing, and faithfulness. I asked God why He had led me to this story. He revealed to me that my father and mother wounds needed healing, but He chose to deal with my mother wounds first. He reminded me of what He said earlier by Him staffing my life and revealed that Ms. B was who He'd chosen to help heal and impart motherly nurturing into me. It was confirmation for me because I had been wondering why my mother couldn't be like Ms. B. I had begged God many times to help me understand why and He gave me clarity one day after spending quality time with Ms. B.

He revealed to me that His help doesn't always come packaged the way I expected. In other words, the nurturing I never received from my natural mother, He had imparted in Ms. B! The light bulb came on! That was why I was so drawn to her. God had sent her to impart many of the missing mothering pieces I never had. God showed me that He has so many ways of giving His children what they need, and He will choose whomever and whatever to get His will fulfilled in their lives. From that day on, there was a name exchange in my heart, from Ms. B to Momma B! She had no idea what had taken place inside of me.

A weight was lifted, I called her to share what God had revealed and she embraced it, while assuring me that her intention was to never replace my mom but to be a mom to me in the Spirit. I respected her concern. Any time a narcissist takes wind of someone else being available for you it will send them into rage and jealousy because they need your supply for their own use. When God gives you a revelation about your deliverance and process it will not make everyone happy, but you must still embrace it with a convinced inner faith that it will work out for your good. This was about my healing not the needs of others.

In the story of Naomi and Ruth, Naomi had lost her two sons and had no other sons to give to Naomi and Orpah. Orpah ran back to her familiarity and Ruth choose to stick with Naomi; she really didn't know why, but she felt like Naomi had something to impart in her even though Naomi begged her to go back because she had nothing to offer. They both had no idea what they had to offer each other, but as the relationship unfolded, revelation was revealed. Like Naomi and Ruth, our relationship blossomed, and I now knew she was the mother who had been assigned to me by God. Soaking up the wisdom birthed out of the pain of her experience, liberated mine.

In my journey of processing, I was dating a guy, one of several actually, when I met Momma B, but I wasn't really forthcoming about the relationship when we first met. We would often have conversations about men and how I should carry myself as woman of God... and why this and why that. One day I called her "ugly" crying about a raggedy relationship with a guy. I could hardly get the words out. She gently said, "Come on over and let me teach you how to date." I drove an hour away in desperation for a mother touch. I was so sick of myself and this continual cycle my heart was in.

I arrived, and like a mother she embraced me while I balled in her bosom. She held and fed me naturally then spiritually. She began to show me in the Word where it said that my life is not my own, and that I was bought with the price of Christ's death on the cross. And how God loved me enough to allow everything I attempt to put together to fall apart so that He could put me on the potter's wheel and rebuild, re-staff, redeem and restore my life. Her Titus anointing was pouring out on me as she sternly shared with me that my body was the temple where the Holy Spirit lived and no one else should be occupying that space before marriage. She said you have to decide to stop being the doormat for men to wipe and smear their mess; it only leads to disappointment. That day she encouraged me to build my faith by hearing and obeying the word.

From that day we had ongoing one-on-ones over the course of several months and scales began to fall off my eyes; my perspective on life, myself and my past mistakes all changed. My spiritual muscles built up stamina enough to where I could say no to opportunities that were not good for my growth. It's easy to just tell people to stop doing what they are doing but without revelation, change is nearly impossible. The word says in all your getting, get an understanding. When there's no understanding of a thing there no possibility for the mind to change. Not knowing is one thing but willful ignorance is another. I had a bit of both. Some truth had been revealed to me, but it was simply hard to submit it to God.

Momma B poured into me for hours and then we took a break. We dug into the word more, then rested and ate. We did that until the next day when I woke up, I felt like a truck load of bricks had been lifted off my back as if I had not slept in years. Her home was a place of hiding and refuge, a place of refueling; to gain strength for the journey ahead. That day bonded our relationship for years to come. God used her mother mantle to impart into me for years. She was the bridge who God used to help me crossover and enter gaining a proper perspective of who God created me to be. A major part of my womanhood was cultivated through the wisdom, love, and patience of Momma B. He sent me my own midwife.

Just as God used Naomi to impart into Ruth, the same was exemplified in our relationship. When Ruth made the commitment to Naomi by declaring to her, "Wherever you go, I go." There was an inner knowing in Ruth, even though she had no idea what it was, that Naomi possessed something that she needed, regardless of what Naomi thought or felt about what she had to offer. Ruth chose to stick by Naomi's side; to press toward the future to see what would unfold, instead of choosing to go back to her sunken place; her past. Ruth knew what her home had to offer after her husband died; absolutely nothing that would contribute to her future. She grabbed faith by the horns and trusted that her future had to offer something greater than her past pain.

In the same way, Momma B taught me many lessons about my womanhood, during my single journey. For example, I was dating a guy for a few months and it was a mess from day one. He had no car, no job no plan, no nothing. I seemed to attract dudes who needed more mothering than I did. Blinded by my own neediness. I found myself enabling them and depleting me.

One time, there was this guy I was dating who I had grown quite frustrated with because he contributed nothing to this so-called relationship. Momma B drove up for her hair appointment and saw him sleeping in my car — waiting for another opportunity for me to supply his needs. She called me outside and asked me why was this dude in my car asleep while I was in there working my butt off? She was upset that he continued to ask me for money to fund his foolishness. She said, "Daughter, you need to cut him and cut him quickly! He's dead weight! I love you and want the best for you!"

As she gave me the hard truth, my eyes began to sweat; not solely because I didn't want to hear it, but because I knew it was the truth and I was exhausted by carrying the unnecessary baggage. I just needed confirmation to end it. I know that sounds crazy, but scapegoats are groomed to not say "no" or not to defend themselves because of narcissistic abusers who are masters at silencing your voice through intimidation and false responsibility. I responded to her with a sense of shame but agreed.

All that day I had asked God to give me an exodus out of the mess I had created. I knew right then that this was my way out. I sucked up the tears and returned to work with one goal in mind — don't let the weekend end with him having any access to my life.

In route to taking him home, he asked me for help to pay his child support. I couldn't even speak. When I tell you, I was so done! I couldn't wait until I dropped his ___ off at his mama's house. As soon as he dropped that second foot on the ground, I burned rubber out of there. God gave me a way of escape by way of putting a stop to all of this foolery. We laugh about that now, but she was hot about it back then.

Other pivotal moments of her wisdom played a vital role in teaching me discipline, boundaries, and structure to and in my development as a woman. She taught me the importance of keeping my body until marriage, and how God can give you a renewed virginity just as he gives us a renewed life in Him. When I found out I was having a baby, I went through some very heavy emotional depression before, and intense postpartum afterwards. She nurtured, prayed, and spoke life into me. It seemed as if she always had a ready word. When I had my daughter, my parents came to see their granddaughter in the hospital but left after a short time. A few days later my husband was at work and couldn't get away so he called my parents to see if they would take us home from the hospital. They both gave some shallow excuse for not being able to pick us up. My husband called Mama B and with no hesitation, she rushed to retrieve us. I don't know why I expected my parents to show up for me but to not show up for their granddaughter was beyond me. It still made me angry and embarrassed for a long time after.

We were always there for each other. Her car broke down on the interstate around 2 a.m. one morning and she called us after a policeman refused to give her a lift. She made her way to a store that was in a highly drug infested area and she was in tears. We immediately drove to get our mom. When she saw us, she cried in my husband's arms as he comforted her. We brought her home and cared for her.

She and her family have been a consistent positive influence in our daughter's life. My daughter calls her Nana and their bond was birthed from the time she was born and I'm forever grateful. Not only did God answer my prayer for my maternal wounds but He knew, before I did, that my daughter would need a Nana in her life. To this day I'm eternally grateful for every seed of wisdom planted in me. It produced a healthy harvest.

# Chapter 16

## The Reality of My Brokenness

L et's look at the word **Brokenness**: Reduced to fragments, fractured, torn not functioning properly, out of working order, weakness in strength and spirit.

When seeking healing from my brokenness, I had to first come into agreement of just how deep my inner wounds were. Just like you can tell how old a tree is by its roots, accessing the age of my abuse, over thirty years, was a strong indication of how deep rooted my toxic spiritual roots were. That alone revealed just how much I would have to fight to come out of the stigma and sting of narcissistic abuse. It also discouraged me at first because I didn't think I had the strength to fight for anything. I was depleted.

Accepting it, facing it, admitting it, submitting to it, and not running from it, were a lot of big pills to swallow. However, the Holy Spirit, coupled with God's word and wisdom, gave me the peace, strength, and comfort to embrace this process. I had to trust His process of knowing how to mend my life back together by using the broken pieces of my journey to heal and set me free.

He reminded me of Psalm 34:18 (NIV) where it says, "The Lord is close to the brokenhearted and saves those who are crushed in spirit."

Narcissistic abuse is sent from hell with the intent to crush you beyond repair by driving you insane. The enemy uses diabolical spirits that whisper constant, repetitive lies in your ear with the hopes of you believing every one of them. But God's says He's the closest when we're in our lowest. A broken spirit is what is produced when a person's heart, emotions and mental health have been so crushed until there is no desire to have a life worth living.

Let me share with you some of the root issues of my brokenness: *rejection, fear of rejection, disapproval, perfectionism, an orphan spirit, fear, and anger.*

G rowing up I knew I was rejected but I had no idea I had been rejected from the womb. It was deeper than I could imagine. It wasn't until my early forty's I became aware of what I call *"utero rejection"*. Studies show that a baby knows whether the mother is bonded to it or not or wanted or not. The womb of the mother shapes what the child thinks of himself/herself. Whether the womb, the incubator, is embracive or rejective, the baby knows. Whenever the mother or even the father doesn't want the baby, or even wishes for a certain sex, the spirit of rejection directly attaches itself to the baby while still in the womb. Despite inward or outward rejection, this spirit can, and will, shape every emotion and mental attitude within the soul and spirit of the baby. This brought so much clarity to me as to why my mom never bonded with me from a baby. It took the light of God's word to illuminate the truth in order to dispel the deceptive lies the enemy had tricked me into believing — I was unworthy, I was not valuable, I was the reason everyone else was unhappy, I'm never good enough. Whatever the mother goes through it transfers to the baby.

If there's a bloodline spirit of rejection It can and will continue to flow thru the bloodline until someone recognizes it, confronts it, heal from it, and expose the truth of it.

**Abandonment** to leave behind, to withdraw, disregard, to vacate.

I didn't realize I had deep abandonment issues until my early twenties — well into my thirties. The spirit of abandonment is the cousin of rejection and they often work as a team.

This dynamic duo involves never giving grace to others for being human — one of the revelations I had to learn about my mom. Abandonment requires deep inner healing from the lie that you're nothing but trash. The spirit of abandonment dehumanizes people into unworthiness and despair. It then attaches itself to the identity, the soul and spirit of a person where they can only see themselves as a reject, someone not worth of redemption. Rejection shouts, you're unwanted, abandonment shouts I'm never good enough. They team up together to oppress the mind and spirit. Many times, the fear of abandonment is the fuel behind promiscuity and/or the reason why so many stay in an abusive relationship. I had attached to many soulish relationships for years because of the fear of feeling the pain of being abandoned again — the results always ended in more abandonment.

Abandonment is a bit different from rejection because its damage is to your spirit rather than your soul. It kills your will to live. It forces you to agree and confess things such as "I want to die", "This will never get better." The word proclaims death and life is in the power of the tongue. Abuse is more spiritual because the evidence from it is invisible. Narcissistic abuse is again, what I call an "invisible wound" in which the untrained eye will never detect it.

***People -Pleasing*:** the strong desire to fit in the status quo.

People pleasing stems or is a branch of the fear of being rejected or abandoned. It constantly eats at your conscious intimidating you into not standing up for yourself or fearing someone's disapproval. In the narcissistic family structure, as the scapegoat you're trained to say no to yourself and yes to the abuser, which in turn pleases them and never you. You're pressured to dumb down who you are in order to make others happy at your expense. The desperation of wanting to be accepted, defended, protected, connected, and loved by my mom shaped my thinking into accepting things and people into my life that only took and never gave. This dysfunctional character trait breeds deeper depths of rejection, emotional abandonment, and people-pleasing. It teaches you to not to value healthy self-care. You become the doormat for others. People-pleasing is an invisible prison that's often overlooked.

***Scapegoat*:** a person or group made to bear the blame for others; fall guy; a doormat.

Leviticus 16:22 shows us that a scapegoat is an animal that is ritually burdened with the sins of others and then driven away into the wilderness.

Sad to say, but that's exactly, what the reality of my life as a scapegoat felt like. I had no inclination I was marked as the *"black sheep"* of and for the family. Scapegoats are chosen by the abuser(s) in the family to be the doormat, burden barrier and reason why everything goes wrong with the family.

Ancient societies took the term scapegoat from when they chose a goat to represent the sins of others. By sending the goat out as the sacrificial offering it represented a clean slate for the people. Though narcissistic parents never bond with their children they are well aware of which child is strong and weak, independent-minded, or vulnerable to anything. They focus on the one who's the strongest and the greatest threat. The one who doesn't go with the flow, the one who stands for truth, the one that asks questions no one wants to answer. Scapegoats are forced into living a wilderness life which signifies the strength and fortitude that is built within them. Even though ostracized from family, the emotional and mental abuse was what God used to build me for what He was calling me to.

Scapegoats are deliverers but often times they don't even know it until they have disconnected from the abuse and began healing.

*Muzzle*: to restrain from speech; to stifle; to gag; to restrict; silence; to shut down

Being under such tumultuous strain as a scapegoat, this dark spirit strips you of your voice. It beats you down bit by bit until it gains absolute control over your response. Parental narcissist within the family dynamic is a master at silencing the voice of the scapegoat by way of muzzling them and in covering family secrets. Your identity is stripped for the sake of forcing you to bow down and submit to the abuse. Gaslighting is one of their main tactics.

The parental abuser has no capacity to empathize with anyone but themselves.

I'm still not where I want to be, but I'm thankful that I am not where I used to be. Silence has been shattered and the muzzle has been stripped. My voice is being heard through the pages of my story in hopes that it will bring awareness and help deliver others out of bondage.

> *Fear:* a distressing emotion aroused by impending danger, evil, pain, etc.; the feeling or condition of being afraid; despair, anxiety, panic; timidity; phobia

Fear plays a strong driving force in the dynamics of a dysfunctional family. It is a controlling spirit that intends to intimidate you into shrinking back in the face of change, opposition, or struggle. Fear was transferred to me in the womb and as a bloodline spirit I've struggled with it my entire life. God never promised us fear wouldn't present itself, but He did give us authority over it. Growing up, fear imprisoned me, even when things were calm; it hovered in the atmosphere.

Fear is a spirit from hell sent to paralyze God's people and to deem them motionless and unfruitful. I've always known that fear was a dark spirit because of how it dominated my every thought, decision, and responses. I didn't know the origin. This may seem simple, but it's huge to a person who has experienced narcissistic abuse; the invisible wound is hard to detect through an untrained eye.

Fear and guilt tactics are needed to keep children and adult children at bay and under control. I learned fear can be annihilated and destroyed by the authority of God's Word every time it raises its ugly head. Fear makes you unfused, navigating thru life in a smog. Living life, through the lens of emotional abuse teaches you to not trust yourself in anything, so you succumb to just about anything. Though, fear still rises to challenge me, I've learning how to respond and take authority over it. This is a tough spirit to overcome but through perseverance and faith I can be strong and courageous in the face of fear.

**Comparison:** capability of being compared; discrimination, breeds separation, dividing, analyzing

Comparison can breed discrimination in many structures in our lives, including the family. When parents compare siblings there's constant seeds of competition sown. One or more is favored (golden child), the other devalued (scapegoat) and this creates an unhealthy environment of divisions rather than unity.

God has gifted every person with unique gifts and He never compares His children to each other, but rather encourages us to use our gifts to expand the Kingdom and not to compare. Unlike our Creator, narcissistic parents compare their children to each other, sometimes unknowingly. This doesn't negate the fact that it's destructive to its core though. With a narcissistic parent, siblings are rarely encouraged to be each other's keeper; instead, they are emotionally disconnected from each other due to the seed of discord brewing while growing up.

Family discussions, reasoning, connecting with one another was rarely a reality in our home. Yes, we ate together, had holiday dinners together, went to church together, but feelings were never respected or acknowledged. In contrast we were taught to repress, stuff, and hide everything. There were days of laughter and rare moments of listening to my dad's funny stories of how he grew up, however, talking about feelings was a no-no! I realized, as an adult that narcs have no empathy for how others feel nor are they in touch with their own feelings.

Comparison has been a tough one to overcome. Some days it raises its ugly head. I've come to realize that the spirit of comparison is sent to steal your joy and keep your attention directed on others instead of what God has for you!

# Chapter 17

## Unmasking the Real Me

*Unmask*: to strip the mask or disguise from; to reveal the true character of; to appear in true nature; expose to the light; unveil.

M y encounter with Christ will always get the glory for my unmasking journey. Before I was in my mother's womb my Heavenly Father knew me, named me, and predestined me for the plan He had for me, I was masked with God's purpose and creativity. Upon my arrival into the earth the enemy, through trauma and bloodline curses, attacked the very essence of who God created me to be by attempting to re-mask me with a false identity.

A mask is a counterfeit version of who you are. What's under the mask is the true version of yourself whether good, bad, or indifferent. It is designed to disguise a person's natural personality appearance to conform to social pressures, abuse, behaviors, etc. Since the beginning, back to Adam and Eve, we've learned to mask and hide from the nakedness of ourselves; it's an automatic response in the effort to cover ourselves from missing the mark, the abuse of this world and from facing God.

Unknowingly, I entered this world with a mask I never knew existed. As I walked through life, I found myself hiding behind multiple masks in the effort of guarding myself from future abuse rooted out of parental narcissistic abuse. The more I navigated through life, toxicity drew to me like a magnet and the masks duplicated.

Trying to unmask yourself in your own might is an insurmountable task that only leads to more bondage. I found myself one day, laid out on the floor pleading for the help of the Lord to unmask me and deliver me from the fear of facing that one unfamiliar person — *me*! God did it but I had to be a co-laborer with Him in my process. He revealed to me that His will and my will cannot reign; one must go! Guess who won?

I had several areas I had to **unmask**: accept that my life *is not* my own; and that wearing the mask of shame, rejection, abandonment, fear, people-pleasing and false identity created the perfect place for hiding. To be candid, I never enjoyed the weight of this mask, but I was too fearful of the vulnerability it would require to not wear it. Abuse teaches you to trust your ways, not because they're effective, but because they're familiar. I had to relinquish the fact that my life was my own and I knew what was best for me and this is my body. He de-masked me from all my ideology thru this scripture:

Galatians 3:13-18 (AMP) says, *Christ purchased our freedom and redeemed us from the curse of the law and its condemnation by becoming a curse for us... in order that the blessing of Abraham might also come to the Gentiles (me, us) so that we all could receive the promise of the Holy Spirit through faith.*

When I forfeited my right of being the captain of my own ship in exchange for Gods leadership, He not only became "Savior" but "Lord" over my life. He told me I no longer needed that mask. Forfeiting my right to be right was scary. This was an uncomfortable process, but it was necessary.

Trust is a *must* in the process: Abuse teaches you to not trust anyone but yourself. In fact you're so broken, bruised and drained, you can't even perceive the fact that it took trust when you entered abuse and will take trusting God and his co-laborers to help heal you post abuse.

So, He came for the second mask! Shedding the mask of wanting things my way while desiring Gods approval was a joke. This process required an exchange of my perspective for the Father's.

Process takes time to come into the truth of unraveling the way we've done and thought about things all our lives. It often requires deserting experiences and thought patterns from our past. Oftentimes, our upbringing reveals beliefs, traditions, and fables that we've deemed as truth and were taught to live by. Many particles of our broken childhood and adult experiences have been lodged in the corners of our hearts and thoughts, taking up residence illegally.

Invisible doors have been opened for these spirits of deception and error to come in. I remember clearly during one of my frustrated seasons wondering why things weren't working out. "Why is God not hearing me? Man, this is for the birds!" I had a whole tantrum about how I could've done this or that then God led me to

Isaiah 55:8-9 tell us, *"For my thoughts are not your thoughts, neither are your ways my ways, declares the Lord. For as the heavens are higher than the earth, so are my ways higher than your ways and my thoughts higher than your thoughts…"*

Revelation hit me in the head like a hammer, and I was challenged by God, not the devil, to continue fighting to have my way or… trust the God of my process. Y'all, this was a loaded revelation. God's process looks like it's taking too long. His thoughts and ways about your specific process will be different than everyone else's. He's a Father and He knows us before we are in our mother's womb. He stitched us together. He chose our destiny. He knows when we're about to make a dumb decision way before it enters our minds. He knows how many hairs are currently on our head. He knows which one of His children needs more patience than the other. He knows our potential before we do. He knew you were going to go through the pain of rape, narcissistic parenting, incest, abuse, and abandonment. He's an all-knowing God!

I have come into agreement that God is not, and will not, think and do things like me. His ways are higher, and His thoughts are above brilliant. The way He masterfully teaches us to trust Him, as He sits back and allow the very situations, we think are killing us, to help prune, develop and mature us. God gives us an opportunity to trust Him even when everything looks dead. In the natural, none of it makes sense, but I am still learning, that on this journey with God that He uses the pressures, disappointments, anger and frustrations to show us what's in us, to purify us in the fire of life and to prove to the naysayers that He holds His children in the palm of His Hand and rescues them when everyone else counted them out. Truly trusting God takes a daily decision to walk away or stick it out with the God who is in control of it all.

## Repentance

The bruises and pain from trauma sowed anger and confusion at God for giving me parents that abused me and left me mentally and emotionally dead. I couldn't understand. I couldn't grasp the fact that He created me for others to take advantage of me. I couldn't grasp the fact that there was a purpose in all of it.

This mask covered (inner) resentment towards my parents, anger, ill thoughts, dislike, promiscuity, idolatry, perversion, unworthiness, emotional torment and all the emotions attached to trauma, I had all this hidden in the corridors of my heart masked with an external happiness.

God told me to take it off. But I still tried to pretend not to hurt, pretend not to be angry and pretend I was all good. God showed me in His word that I must repent with my mouth. Confession is good for the soul because it releases the spiritual poisons of the soul and challenges you to turn in another direction. Give the weight of that mask to the One who made you. I could not honor God in anything I endeavored without repenting from my sins. It liberated my soul. It freed me from harboring a burden I was never meant to carry

## Unforgiveness

No matter how we slice it, when we ask God to be Lord over our life, that includes our emotions, will and mind. Life can throw some tough blows that shakes the very foundation of our lives. Many unlawful, wrong, and abusive acts are absolutely justifiable and understandable. However, in order for us to be totally free from bondage of sin and death we have to forgive the offender, the rapist, the narcissist, the murderer and leave vengeance to Him.

Forgiveness is not about the offender but you(me). The depth of my abuse, the invisible wound of parental narcissism was an injustice that had nothing to do with what I did but everything to do with what God allowed to happen. This mask of unforgiveness was a doozie. In my ignorance, I viewed forgiving my parents and sibling as them getting away with the abuse unpunished. I learned to see it through the eyes of Christ. We have not always been the victim; we've missed the mark as well and we need grace.

Daddy God reminded me of the principle of sowing and reaping. If I sowed grace, I would receive grace. God challenged me to stop pretending I've forgiven when I really haven't. Forgiveness is an intentional act of obedience and leaving the rest to God. Forgiveness doesn't always mean you have to sit at the table with the abuser and become subject again but more about the cleanliness of your heart submitting to doing it Gods way and leaving vengeance to Him. He will repay but His way not ours.

## Inner Healing, Deliverance & Counseling

This dynamic trio is a must when it comes to unmasking. For growth to take place we endure this process. Many times, we deem this process unnecessary. We think salvation and repentance is enough and it is in the spirit, However, these three components teaches us to unlearn wrong thinking, come out of agreement with inner vows we've made to ourselves and getting the strongholds cast out so that inner healing can began.

All three are vital to us being whole. Being whole is what God desires us to be; it pleases him. When we're whole, we live through life without bleeding on others including ourselves. Some of us have gone through some traumatic, brutal things in life and it has left you maimed. You are alive but crippled. You're disabled in the spirit realm. You're not operating at full capacity and when you refuse to add these components to your life it does you, your gifts, and your relationships a disservice.

In my perspective, not embracing one without the other is like calling on God without the whole trinity, the Holy Spirit and Jesus! This is more about self-care than it is about what others say.

God challenged me to take it off. I cannot tell you it was easy, but it brings a level of healing, maturity, and freedom like you've never experienced.

## Become a Kingdom Seeker

We live in a world where everything we desire is in hands reach. The buffet of life will present itself will many pleasurable things and people, however, under the canvas of flattery you'll find yourself laying in the bed of many, sometimes hard consequences due to our inner desires. This world is a master at casting the bait of temptation and destruction persuading you to take the bait called pleasures, whispering in your ear saying, "Nothing will happen", "You only live once, so live it up. Do whatever you want."

As a believer who's now given my life over to the Lordship of my Father, I had to get a new seek! My old seek only led me to the pleasures of my flesh and the word of God tells us to put no trust in your flesh! My flesh could no longer be trusted. Flesh is beautiful, flesh is handsome, flesh is intelligent and flesh can be downright stupid, but flesh is, and flesh will lead you down paths of unrighteousness and cannot be used as a GPS to the perfect will of God.

Matthew 6:33 (AMP) says, *"But first and most importantly seek (aim at, strive after) his Kingdom and righteousness (His way of doing and being right— the attitude and character of God), and all these things will be given to you also."*

My seek changed y'all! My flesh no longer had preeminence over God's will. Do I struggle in some areas still? You bet! However, it no longer has the driver's seat. I had to learn not to allow my flesh to overtake the will of the Father and His wisdom knowingly. Whether pursuing my dreams, my plans, or desiring to be married, seeking out my future or asking Him what season I'm in, etc., my seek had to be measured by two questions: Is what I desire Kingdom-driven or flesh-driven? And when I'm not sure I do nothing until I get peace about it. Will what I desire bring God glory or misrepresent Him?

I started practicing this with little things. Is the music I listen to pleasing to my Father? Is what's coming out of my mouth exalting or controlling? Was how I treated the waitress at the diner pleasing to God or did I make her feel like a slave while serving me? Or was stealing paper from my job without permission honorable to God? The more I strived to honor and represent God in all that I did, the more I experienced inner peace. Doors began to open for me, favor began to follow me, and my character changed without me saying a word. Did it happen overnight? Not at all. Having a new seek changed my perspective on how I viewed everything. Instead of reacting, I learned to be proactive. A new seek challenged me to view things from the mountain top instead of the valley. You will begin to see the good, the lesson in everything. Though it's tough to seek the message of God in the mess sometimes, it is vital. A new seek calls me to maturity and stands back to see how I choose to handle it. Some things that once mattered, no longer matter, I learned to let go. Seeking righteousness and doing things the Kingdom way is always rewarding.

**Faith**

Hebrews 11:6 (AMP) without faith it's impossible to (walk with God and) please him, whoever comes near to God must believe that God exists and that He rewards those who (earnestly and diligently) seek Him.

Without faith, my walk with the Father is all in vain. I had to come to grasp with the truth — no faith, no future; not the one He has chosen for me. I was afraid to have faith for fear of God not coming through, So I would keep it at bay for quite some time until I had gained enough leverage in my walk with Christ to know that I wanted God's perfect will for me and not His permissible will. Everything permissible is not good for us. Some things may not necessarily be a bad thing but it just not good for me! Everything I trusted God for in my younger life until now, it was done by Faith.

You cannot expect anything without faith. Faith is the landing strip for takeoff and landing. Faith is the platform in which we allow God to operate through us and demonstrate His wonderous works to us and others. Faith breeds expectancy. Why serve and submit to a God and never expect anything from Him? That gives no hope. The motive should never be to serve Him to get things, but to serve Him sacrificially because of who He is and thanking Him for choosing to give us life. After all, it's His breath in our lungs and without it there's no life. Faith is trusting Him to give me a way of escape out of some bad relationships, financially, mentally, emotionally. I've had to have faith in and through it all. My desire is to please Him and that can't be obtained without Faith.

## Prayer

Learning to communicate with God was intimidating. With my fallacious orphan spirit, I viewed everything from the eyes of potential abandonment and fear of doing things wrong. This door was opened when I was a child. Perfection laced with image, were active idols in our household. There was only one way to do something and that was her perfect way. Attempting to communicate with her about anything activated intense anxiety in me because I was used to hearing "No" to everything — without a chance to be heard. I perceived communication as "Do as I say do, not as I do". An orphan is often looked upon as inhuman, nasty, and having no voice. They're often used as slaves to do extremely humiliating tasks. When you grow up in this stern, hard, stoic atmosphere, you grow to not value yourself nor voice. In fact, it's been so long since you heard your voice, you no longer believe you have one.

God came for that too. He compelled me to come to Him; spend time with Him. I was good talking to Him from a distance because that's what I was trained to do and that's what was comfortable. If it even it sounded like their response was a disapproval, I would go into a shell and automatically silence myself. Orphans view everything from a low place. From a place of no expectancy. From a place of poverty, brokenness, and darkness.

I was afraid of being in the light of anything; even the camera! Yes, the cam, fam! Can you believe it? Miss talk-a-lot. Miss Social

Butterfly. Miss I love people? I hated taking pictures and I never knew why until God revealed it to me as I was writing this book.

Yes! For nearly forty years I had no idea why I ran from taking pictures. While communing with God in His presence, one day I asked Him. He reminded me that my mom hated taking pictures and I never knew why. There was a connection. He wanted to reveal something to me. This thing was generational. He revealed to me that my lens, how I viewed myself, always came from a low and shattered view. My esteem was low, my courage was low, my hope low; everything was low. I would cringe when asked to take pictures because afterwards, people would say how beautiful it was, how chic it was, "You're such an inspiration to me," but I would absolutely pick myself apart. I honestly believed my lot in life was the background, the cheerleader for everyone else, the exhorter for everyone else; I was fine right where I was.

A slave approaches his master with no eye contact and head dropped low, begging for left over crumbs and they're accustomed to not asking for more for fear of harsh punishment. From the Master's perspective, he has a right to do whatever he desires with you without consequences. A dictator instills fear early so that it communicates to others, "Don't even think about thinking for yourself or outside the parameters of the rules." Communicating with God revealed that to me, and it has been liberating. When you see me take pictures now, I hear God's voice telling me, "Do it scared. Do it anyway. Do it until you walk into your God-given confidence."

With this being said, when God began to woo me into spending time with Him, my automatic response would be, "Why would you want to spend time with me in your face? I've done so much wrong in my life. I don't deserve being in your pure presence. I'm too dirty and shameful." Satan loves when we're afraid to spend time in the presence of the Father. Why? Because in His presence there's fullness of joy, in His presence scales fall off our eyes; our sight is clearer, our hearing is keener and our spirits, broken hearts and concerns, are poured before Him as an offering. This is the place where our Father comes to see about His children. He loves us and is concerned about what concerns us.

The day I read these passages of scriptures, the altitude of my perspective shifted higher. When I read it, I felt the breath of God blow into me from the pages and felt a new level of awakening in this area. I'd been operating as a slave driven orphan, from a child well into my forties. I had no idea what had been so bound in this area. It was like the woman with an issue of blood. I was existing but never living. I was bleeding and didn't know how to stop it from happening.

Galatians 4:4-7 (MSG) reads, *"But when the time arrived that was set by God the father, God sent His son, born of a woman, born under the conditions of the law so that he might redeem those of us who have been kidnapped by the law."*

Thus, we have been set free to experience our rightful heritage. You can tell for sure that you are now fully adopted as his own children because God sent the Spirit of his Son into our lives crying out, "Papa! Father!"

Doesn't that privilege for intimate conversation with God make it plain that you are not a slave, but a child? And if you are a child, you're also an heir, with complete access to the inheritance.

This was extremely liberating.

I cried for hours.

I realized that I had been living beneath my potential and birthright. I never knew I had an inheritance to look forward to. I found out that I can see the goodness of the Lord now, on earth, and not wait until I get to heaven. God confirmed it by saying,

"Stop dismissing yourself from the table I've prepared for you."

"Who told you that you don't have a right to be here?"

"Stop being intimidated by the riches at the table; it's your inheritance. Take part and eat!"

When I accepted Christ, I was also adopted as a son (daughter) into the family of God. I no longer had to carry myself as a slave being fearful to communicate to my own creator. My relationship with the Father wasn't perfect, but it was pure. I no longer had to approach my "Daddy" trying to earn my place in His heart when it was already given. He chose me before I chose Him. I no longer felt like I had to do everything with the spirit of perfection before I approached Him. No longer did I feel like everyone else had a special place with Him and not me. I no longer felt the weight of intimidation in His presence like He was this big God in the sky just waiting to hammer me because of every mistake I had made. God is a good Father. He is love and He's full of love; there's nothing we can do to stop him from loving us the way he does. I will never understand why He loves us so much beyond all our faults. His love is everlasting, but His benefits are conditional. Just as an earthly Father, He loves us but will not give us everything we want, when we want it. Communicating with the Father opens up wisdom, strategies, opportunities for Him to comfort, lead and guide us. For us to listen to Him and to just bask in His goodness opens up things that have been locked up for years. Let Him pour out His mysteries to you, He longs to have you in His presence.

# Chapter 18

## The Purpose of it All

**Purpose:** the reason why something exists or is made; an intended or desired result; to resolve; the intent of a thing.

God does nothing without a purpose. Purpose is His DNA. It's his "M.O." It's how He flows. He created purpose itself. He had a purpose for a purpose. Without purpose our mere existence is vague and ineffective. There's a purpose for each animal in the animal kingdom, there's purpose for every insect, there's purpose for the carpet of flowers that arrays an open field, there's purpose for the sun to illuminate the sky during the day and purpose for the moon and stars at night. Everything small and great has a purpose. We have a purpose, and our purposes are unique and are to be used for the glory of God. When God blew breath in us, he also engrafted purpose!

*For in Him all thing were created: things in heaven and on earth, visible an invisible, whether thrones or power or rulers or authorities, all things have been created through him and for him. (Colossians 1:16)*

*I know that you can do all things; no purpose of yours can be thwarted.*
(Job 42:2)

*But the plans of the Lord stand firm forever, the purposes of his heart through all generations.* (Psalms 33:3)

So just as God has a purpose for everything, He has created us for a purpose, as a solution with a plan to use us, the clay and Him, the Potter. We were born to do something in the earth that brings solutions for others and fulfill us simultaneously. The plan is to reveal to us our unique qualities within us and share it with the world. God desires to shoot us out like arrows in the earth. Gods plans and purposes for our lives have been in existence before the foundation of the world and before we were in our mother's womb. So, you see, we may have come out the womb of a woman, but we've been woven with purpose in the womb of God before the beginning of time.

My purpose in the earth has always been in existence, however, I've been unaware for years; throughout my teens, twenties, thirties. By the time I was aware that I have a purpose; I was in my mid-forties. God is the only Master planner I know. We were never meant to just exist but to live vibrant, productive, and rich lives that exudes the very essence of our heavenly father.

All of this sounds grandiose right? My life never reflected any of this in the beginning. My childhood memories, as you've heard throughout my story, wasn't a bowl of peaches, and I could never see God using me for anything. Pain, especially emotional pain, tends to give you no hope of change. It's the mental Alcatraz you can never seem to escape. All the memories, pain, heartache, and abusive word curses never indicated to me that I had a meaningful purpose. The only purpose I saw was to serve as a dumping ground. The Cinderella no one was interested in. The abused soul left swimming in her own blood of pain with no one to assist her. Left to die! And then I was led to this powerful passage of scripture below. God was literally speaking to me right where I was.

*"On the day you were born, your umbilical cord was not cut, you weren't bathed and cleaned up, you weren't rubbed with salt, you weren't wrapped in a baby blanket. No one cared a fig for you. No one did one thing to care for you tenderly in this way. You were thrown out into a vacant lot and left there, dirty and unwashed--a newborn nobody wanted.* (Ezekiel 16:4-5)

*And then I came by. I saw you miserable and bloody. Yes, I said to you, lying there helpless and filthy,* **live!** *And you did. You grew up. You grew tall and matured as a woman, full-breasted, with flowing hair. But you were naked and vulnerable, fragile and exposed.* (Ezekiel 16: 6-7)

*I came again and saw you, saw that you were ready for love and a lover. I took care of you, dressed you and protected you. I promised you* **my** *love and entered the covenant of marriage with you. I, God, the Master, gave my word. You became mine. I gave you a good bath and anointed you with aromatic oils.* (Ezekiel 16: 8-14)

In this passage, God beautifully displays how being born abandoned, rejected and thrown out to die is the perfect picture of beauty to God. You see God is not moved nor threatened by our filthiness. In fact, He is drawn to it. He's the only one who really knows how to accept us in our mess, clean us up, anoint us and call us Queen. His Royalty! The stench of our bloody nakedness is the very component God uses to create a message from a mess and to use us for His glory. Our stories are to bring Him glory and compel others to develop an appetite where they can taste the Lord and see that He's good! He's not afraid to touch the depth of our infirmities, locate the infection and heal the wounds of our souls. He uses the foolish things to confuse the wise.

He uses misfits, such as me, cleans them up and blows His anointing in us and through us. He cleaned me up from the beds of sin, spoke life to me, sent anointed people to help steer me, clothed and covered me, and sent me out. Who says God can't use someone like me, like you, broken, useless and lifeless in the soul? He can use you too. You say prove it? Okay! Let me testify!

Remember earlier in my story I felt like I was drowning in my own infirmity of narcissistic parenting. I know now that my mother (parents) could only parent me from a limited capacity, but at the time I had much resentment, anger, and confusion. I could not understand for the life of me why I was emotionally thrown out to die, naked and ashamed, exposed, being looked upon as the problem child, the outcast, the black sheep and the broken scapegoat. I wore that false crown and mask for years. Adored outwardly and bleeding internally, screaming and no one hearing me; I sort of faded into the identity of what I was born in. A generational curse I never knew existed until it started manifesting later in my life.

So, you asked how God can use:

- A broken, desperate little girl who long for her mother's love and affirmation.

- A rejected teen who knew nothing about herself life other than "keep your dress down and pants up"; a terrified uninformed teen who awakened in her sleep to be molested by a family member only to be blamed for it.
- A young woman who fled from her home searching for peace, acceptance, and love, only to find herself entangled in the bondage of fornication and deep disappointment.
- The high school girl who was mocked for being promiscuous
- The girl who was pregnant at nineteen and was forced by her parents to get rid of it; no discussion, no closure about it.
- A young woman who finds herself years later pregnant again, and after being abandoned by a one-night stand, shamefully aborts the second baby.
- The young woman drowning in the blood of her sin, and who betrayed her friend unintentionally.
- The full-grown woman who tied her life with multiple 'low-lifes'.
- The grown woman whose outer adornment was "chic", but her inner spirit was a "broken little girl" wondering in the wilderness of life.
- The grown woman who the enemy tried to kill her mind while in the womb.
- The woman-child who was betrayed and left unprotected by the first man she ever knew; her father.
- The woman who dodged multiple suicide temptations.

The answer is an absolute *yes*!

God's love is girded by restoration and redemption! He has the power to redeem lost time. What I thought had no life, God resurrected from the dead. We serve a living redeemer and serve one who is a genius in restoring what He allowed to be eaten, so that much glory can come out of a dead thing. When a dead thing meets up with the spoken Word of God, the authority of the Word brings it alive again and it flourishes as if it never missed a beat.

After I allowed God to detox me, gut me, heal me, process me, and deliver me, He rewarded me beyond comprehension. He said now that you've married me and honored the covenant between you and me, you're now ready for what I had in mind the whole time; the benefits of a Queen.

Remember when I said God can make the foolish things confuse the ones who thought they knew it all, the ones who counted you out, the ones who saw you bleeding and left you for dead? Well He sure used my foolish things to confuse those who knew me.

Remember my friend who I betrayed? Well I asked God to restore the relationship, and He did.

I asked God to empty me out and restore me. I needed Him to redeem the time I had lost with fake friends and counterfeit men and make me content in my single season. He did that.

I prayed and asked God to restore my virginity back. He did. God is a miracle working God. In my Spirit I was healed and pure again. When I tell you, He did that "thang"!

Remember the drug dealer, the one who I met through his cousin, and we'd parted ways because of his lifestyle and him not wanting me to get caught up in that? After many years, God brought our paths back together. By this time, he had given his life to Christ while he was in prison. God had placed Him on my heart to pray for him. Shortly after that, I received a phone call from him out of nowhere. He was calling because the Lord had given him instructions to call me to apologize for anything he had done to cause any pain in my life; even though I never felt he had. This was the man that looked out for me and had my back when I didn't even know it. He thought I had gotten married because he heard that I was engaged again. He had no idea that I had broken it off because that second fiancé wasn't God's best for me either.

We became great friends, encouraged one another, prayed with and for each other. The relationship naturally blossomed into a pursuit with the intention to marry me. I didn't take him seriously at first, but when he wrote a letter to my pastor letting her know his intentions to marry me upon his release, I realized he was genuine and was willing to submit to whatever process he had to in order to attain his prize. I was amazingly shocked because I was not used to a man being so straightforward and fighting for me like I was worth something to fight over. He said to me, "He who has nothing to hide, hides nothing." He was going for *The One*!

Upon his release, I reconnected with his family, whom I had known since the nineties. They actually remembered me. I'm still shocked about that! I talked this over with the Lord and my accountability partners, who were Momma B, Dea, and my pastor at the time. My pastor wrote him back and informed him that her response has nothing to do with him being incarcerated but everything to do with his motives. She told him that she will be very protective of her spiritual daughter and will be watching. He kept his word to my pastor; he has never crossed nor dishonored me.

Soon I met his other son and we hit it off well.

Lamar and I got married and have now been married for eighteen years. We have two sons, a daughter and have a brand-new grandson.

God used an ex-big-time-drug dealer from the east side, and a "little ole gal" who grew up on the southside, who was green as an evergreen tree and knew nothing about the streets, to come together for purpose. He knew nothing about authentic love. God knew what we needed to balance each other out. Neither of us have done things perfectly, but I can say we have kept God in the three braided cord, and it has not been broken.

We now happily live in Georgia. God constantly uses us without us even knowing it. We attract singles and broken men and women who admire what God has put together.

I can honestly say that many people counted us out and said it would never work. However, you learn to choose your battles and live your life for Christ, and he rewards those who diligently seek to please Him.

When the adversary comes for the very purpose God called you to, He will give you the *strength*, *strategy*, and a *steadfast spirit* to *triumph* over the *traumas* in your life!

I can now truly testify that my *traumas* became my *triumph*!

# Prophetic Poem

## Your Destiny Awaits

By J.D. Richards

I see someone that's in you
That you don't see yourself.
It's time for you to let her out
Cause you stuck her on the shelf.

I would love to introduce you
Because you deserve to know
That person trapped inside
Wants to show you where to go.

Embrace this time with urgency
Because you don't want to regret
Not stepping out on your plan and purpose
Designed to remove your debt.

You're being called out; can't you hear it?
Come forth you must move fast.
Procrastination will ruin your destination
Step forward, forget the past.

I see someone that's in you,
That you don't see yourself.
You've got to let it out.

So please Ma'am meet yourself!

# About the Author

*Dee Dee Moreland*

Demeatrice "Dee-Dee" Moreland is first and foremost a daughter of the King, Jesus Christ, the wife of an amazing ingenious and industrious husband for eighteen years, the mother of two authentic adult children, one extremely creative teen and one joyous new grandson. A native of Atlanta, Georgia, she loves people, hospitality, and Kingdom agenda. Her passion in everything she does is rooted in advancing the Kingdom of God and wearing His name, not in perfection, but wearing His name well. Her spirit is naturally jovial and joyous; her essence exudes with bringing strong light into dark places by her mere persona.

Dee-Dee often refers to herself as 'Triumphant". This was birthed out of being groomed in an environment that taught her how to mask "Trauma" by way of emotional toxicity, guilt, shame, rejection, perfection, and false identity. Growing up under the pressures of being the perfect PK (preachers' kid) muzzled her voice for years and convinced her that her voice never mattered. This, in turn, kept her bound for over thirty years.

Her tenacious mission now is to eradicate the spirit of deception and lies of the enemy from the minds of God's people, especially women and girls. *"What goes on in this house, stays in this house."* is no longer the compass that directs her life. Her anointing is to snatch God's daughters out of the prison of being the SCAPEGOAT of other people's brokenness, pain and excuses and introduce them to a life of true identity, wholeness and purpose thru the liberty found in Jesus Christ.

You can find out more about Dee Dee at:
www.deedeemoreland.com

I would love for you to follow me on social media at
Facebook: @dee dee moreland
Instagram: @traumavstriumph

Email: fromtraumatotriumph@gmail.com

Made in the USA
Middletown, DE
13 June 2023

32528283R00096